D0827153

PRIVACY POLICY
The Anthology of Surveillance Poetics

Edited by Andrew Ridker

Black Ocean
Boston · New York · Chicago

Copyright © 2014 by Black Ocean
All rights reserved.

To reprint, reproduce, or transmit electronically, or by recording all or part of this manuscript, beyond brief reviews or educational purposes, please send a written request to the publisher at:

Black Ocean
P.O. Box 52030
Boston, MA 02205
blackocean.org

Cover & Graphics by Abby Haddican | abbyhaddican.com
Book Design by Nikkita Cohoon | nikkitacohoon.net

ISBN 978-1-939568-07-6

Library of Congress Cataloging-in-Publication Data

Privacy policy : the anthology of surveillance poetics / ed. Andrew Ridker.
    pages cm
  Includes index.
  ISBN 978-1-939568-07-6
  1. American poetry--21st century. 2. Privacy in literature. 3. Electronic surveillance. I. Ridker, Andrew, editor.
  PS617.P75 2014
  811'.608--dc23
                      2014019642

FIRST EDITION

TABLE OF CONTENTS

[poets organized by social security number]

In the Psychology Department break room at England's Newcastle University, there sits an Honesty Box. Here, forty-eight university staff members are encouraged to contribute funds to the Box in exchange for the gratis tea and coffee. Instructions for payment are posted on a black and white, 148 mm x 210 mm notice at eye level on a cupboard door above the counter on which the Honesty Box sits.

Back in 2006, three Newcastle behavior scientists added an image banner to the payment notice that alternated each week between a pair of eyes and a picture of flowers. The image was posted directly above the suggested prices for tea, coffee, and milk. Contributions remained anonymous and effectively impossible to enforce.

The scientists found that monetary contributions to the Honesty Box increased significantly when a picture of eyes ran atop the notice, with a sharp decrease in contributions during the weeks of floral decoration. The conclusion was clear: the impression of being watched, no matter how obviously false, motivates good behavior.

But poetry is not about good behavior.

This project began in the summer of 2013, a season of disclosures that revealed, beyond a reasonable doubt, that we were living in the Age of Surveillance. It was the summer of Edward Snowden's leaks and of Chelsea Manning's conviction. It was the summer that a doctor in Madrid used Google Glass to broadcast a knee surgery, and the summer that a neighborhood watchman named George Zimmerman was acquitted for the murder of seventeen-year-old Trayvon Martin. It seemed as if the people and institutions charged with giving explanations—pundits, politicians, the justice system—were coming up heartbreakingly short.

I began reaching out to poets, wondering if some sense could be made of all this. They are, after all, our professional observers. The interest in minutiae, the data of our daily lives, is their business. Whitman's catalogues of the things he witnessed were intended to instill a shared experience between writer and reader; you may never have crossed Brooklyn Ferry, but he had, and would relate it to you as best he could in the hopes that you might understand it. The tweet and the cameraphone have made poets of us all—and yet, the Utah Data Center hardly feels like a French salon.

The poems contained herein tackle the topic of surveillance from every conceivable angle. Some pieces are political, others deeply personal. Many are both. There are poems about cameras, mirrors, drones, and the internet. There are also poems about sex, Beyoncé, language, power, Thoreau, horses, and depression. Poems about money, bosses, Hitchcock, mountains, and tinfoil hats.

And the poets. They are from different schools and write in different styles. They have different concerns and preoccupations, and their dates of birth span six decades. So what began as poetic variations on a theme became what you hold in your hands now: a survey of contemporary poetry as it stands today.

There has been a lot of fuss lately—forever, really—about the declining relevance of poetry, its shrinking role in the public sphere. I mention the naysayers only that this anthology may be held up as counterpoint. Here are over sixty of our finest living poets—yes, living and breathing and writing!—wrestling with the timeless themes of love and trust and knowledge and death through the lens of our present techno-political crisis. This is poetry as it looks in the twenty-first century, and it is looking right back.

—Andrew Ridker

MARY JO BANG

THE STORM WE CALL PROGRESS

Strum and concept, drum and bitterness, the dog
of history keeps being blown into the present—
her back to the future, her last supper simply becoming
the bowels' dissolving memory in a heap before her.
A child pats her back and drones *there-there*
while under her lifted skirt is a perfect today
where a cult of ghost-lovers predicts a rapture
but instead remains to inherit varicose veins,
rubber knickers, douches with bulbs, douches with bags,
girdles in a choice of pink, red or white,
and in rubber, silk or twilled linen, enemas, clysters, oils
balms, and other Benjamin etceteras burrowing
like scabies into the brain's ear as it listens to the click
of the next second coming to an end.

                                  Throughout,
the senseless waste of reaching up to pull down
a machine-made device from the rafters, a beatific
mythical magical deity. Sturm und drang, storm
and stress, turbulence and urge, turmoil and ferment.
A revolution goes right, then wrong. The right falls
in love with an icon. They force the landscape into a box.
They lock the box with the key inside. The aristocracy
is an improbable agent of change. Whispering
is no longer saying out loud, the all-seeing god a brother
grown bigger by another name.
Adv. sadly
He stared sadly at the ruins of his house. *traurig*
Er starrte traurig auf die Ruinen seines Hauses. *sadly*

JOHN ASHBERY

ANDANTE AND FILIBUSTER

Remember last month, when he was saying
doomed lovers' syndrome uproots us all?
They all wanna hear that,
and hanging them out to dry slumpingly caresses
the center for new needs, and we'll stiffen some near
the walled city and find 100 per cent electricity of the vote.

(Not sure about *that*.) Funny you should ask.
We got a small grant to have the house inspected and
as a result of that discovered a small crack
leading from the front door to the basement.
Much thinner air here, although the nation's salt and pepper
sprinkle the neighborhood. Hose her down. Keep trying
to creep out, test ingot possibilities.
Recently in the stores I spotted
preppy garbage. Grew a ten-gallon hat shopping
in the ruins, how it feels around
the edges—something you do for a moment. Brutally
obnoxious, I like to know who's coming and going
and not be bothered. (Promised

to wake him up in July.) Still not doing
anything to incur our attention?
Then you have followed all what we have to say.
Cough it up—little green cross-eyed slots.
No bricks. Just mortar. Ready. Ready for a takeover.
The catalpas of reconciliation wilt,
proving, if little else,
why a good presentation matters.

MATTHEW ROHRER

SOME PEOPLE

Some people don't know
how to be in public
they don't know everyone
is reading their mind
they shove their bag
in my face
to stand in a certain
way a way that's
out of date
they come from
the very top of a pumice isle
or volcano hut
I no longer wear
my American president t-shirt
and my mind
is folded in on itself
on the metro
there is a thing
they think I am
which is very great & terrible
and am not
under surveillance I am
like listening in
on a tree

HARMONY HOLIDAY

CAN YOU READ MY MIND

White flags pitched in the lawn like sad seeds, the flecks of blue and red blinking in the wind/ innuendo is a close word, it touches my tongue with perfect nuance and gives none away, like the tom in atom minus the uncle and blow-up and Antonioni with subtitles and a bowl a fluffy green grapes, a counter-commons, a shoulder full of suntan/ or that clandestine-for-leverage answer muttered across cultures as songs or cult birds/blackbirds and Donald Byrds and to have gathered all of the memories of your own racism into a guilt that manifests as phrases like *I love Motown,* or, *I love Detroit, or some of my best lies are black and blue, and true too,* stadium acoustics like the anthem in Marvin Gaye's parched bible fraying beside a barrel/Pride is truth's stiffest rival after shame and blood and everything else besides subtlety and re-written creation myths. Like that time I won my own heart in a dance, something about how I could glide through the air and land in a split— made me a technology I wanted to caress and witness/forever: where the anniversary party is this quiet, candlelit, almost vigil punctuated by a crude exhilaration marked with the thrill of survival, ritual, renewal, a power stronger than itself— is love— but that's so trite on nationalism and good grass I almost won't admit it until it's tragic or a some kind of risk or gasp or actually happening and impossible in the same matter-of-fact, like those invisible stars flickering as soon as you look away, tricking you into having mercy on yourself

HE'S A RUNNER

For some, the anxiety becomes charisma. You know you've been spotted like a dalmatian/hysteria/numb, nigga playing god or artman/atman/fugitive/furtive/figurative/urge to give or even gather the tiny eternity of a chasm where fame and anonymity shadow this black american life like a missing language/myth or karmic backlash or the tangle from django to shango, Griot, growl, row of owls but one treehouse on the perch to signal purchase or that those roving eyes are to scale or for sale and forever. My map to the new world is through the foot which was the drum in the field which trusts the run/don't kneel/ to mean, to me, to medium — romance, which these days is about disappearing and in the film I'm making it's a black entertainer's main thing, remember backwards, lack words, excess words, words that are drums, words that beat me, words that beat me to it, words I beat you with or for or forefather words or for example, just 8 lantered minutes of montage of black men and women running, from the cops, from their mothers, from their wives, from their husbands, from their mistresses, from their masters, and re-masters, from their children, from the confessions, from their triumphs, from the sun gods, from the humming neon of progress and slow change, from the gold chain, from the gold medal, from the training, from the narcissism of differences small and large, in the rain, from the rain, to the rain, tainted love, from the urge to run, from themselves—And the final shot, where it all converges, a spotlight with no one in it and do you get too poignant or make a subtle shift in pitch to reach the place that's neither ironic nor overly-earnest which is where the imagination makes us real to ourselves on either side of time and space/intangible and certain and chimes jingling in the race toward nirvana   calm as invisible camels   calm as a blues echo in the footsteps of an iambic soldier, picturing the swift jab of our survival as he runs from out of no where—

CACONRAD

SECURITY CAMERAS AND FLOWERS DREAMING THE ELEVATION ALLEGIANCE

A (Soma)tic Poetry Ritual
for Susie Timmons

From Walnut & Broad St. to Walnut & 19th I stopped for every security camera. Philadelphia watches us always, FUCK YOU WATCHING US ALWAYS!! Several cameras in one block, I took notes, it was noon it was twelve just as I wanted it to be. I took notes for the poem, notes notes notes.

A little basket of edible flowers: nasturtiums, roses, pansies, I eat pansies, I LOVE pansies small buttery purple lettuce!! At each security camera I paused, looked into the camera, DIRECTLY IN THERE and stuck my tongue inside a flower. Flicked it in and out, in and out, flicking, licking, suckling blossoms. A security guard asked *"What the fuck are YOU DOING?"* I replied, "I'M A POLLINATOR, I'M A POLLINATOR!!" This was the only thing I was allowed to say for the duration of the security camera pollination application, "I'M A POLLINATOR, I'M A POLLINATOR!!" I took notes, took many notes, and the notes became a poem titled, "I WANT TO DO EVERY / THING WRONG JUST ONCE"

I WANT TO DO EVERY THING WRONG JUST ONCE

suddenly we are
a daisy under
the big wheel
throw it out to the batter leave it up to the outfield
the umpire sees how I divide you from me
you have no choice over the
weak notes in the song
you think I'm afraid
of course I am
I'm disgusted chopping us in two
will it help to
kill the one who
hypnotizes you?
we can try
we can always try
betting on the better point of quaking
we cap the balding yard with angel wings ancient astronauts
a poetic acuity we have been waiting to carry us away forever
to survive I stayed away from
people who wanted to
kill me (that's
the big secret)
let them jam it
in the back of your
mouth just a quick
police search

MAX HJORTSBERG

DRONE POEM
For Daniel de la Nuez

127830
in the shimmering sun of late afternoon
heat mirage across an empty plain
we knew drone circled overhead

104263
the sweeping shape of the fuselage
propels drone through the sky
above the gala celebration
two stepping a waltz
your evening gown
caressing every curve

N921AU
in the pale winter sky
drone glints in the air
an ice crystal
you watch your breath
cloud with every exhale

083228
there used to be a cloud of dust
in the distance a breathless boy
recently a ringing telephone
now the only sound wind
in the wake of drone

N429GZ
at your backyard barbeque
after one too many
drone watches you lie
down in the grass
arms and legs splayed
like an "X"

N529WP
drone circles
and continues
to circle
so many times
it loses meaning
disappearing

052980
drone of the morning star
flying dawn intruder
the light in your house
a beacon in gray haze

N429CX
in your vegetable garden
plants set roots twisting
around ammo boxes
drone watched you plant
and cultivate with care

111011
drone flies in front of the sun
the morning light streams
in through your windows

N406RQ
in the clouds
drone feels at home
peering into
our garden waiting

N319KW
the poet reclines
in a chaise lounge
pen in hand
cold drink in the other
writing a poem
only drone
gets to read

096598
the snarl of traffic
at the five points
crowds of people walking home
no one waiting for the light
drone in the setting sun
charts the progress
of the blue sedan

103329
the prairie city rises
like mast and rigging
out of the long horizon
drone casts no shadow
over a fallow field

N783PT
at the movies soul music
playing over the closing credits
you tap your foot
drone hears only
wind and propeller
waiting for you to emerge
from the multiplex

N581OZ
pay no attention
to the drone
behind the cloud

169295
painted with eagle feathers
bird sized drone
with avian silhouette
circles awkwardly
like a drunken turkey buzzard

127439
cycloptic eye on the nose of drone
a mind of circuit boards
wire veins a belly full of fuel
your misconstrued thoughts
could be mistaken

N884BK
negotiating a brick labyrinth
drone hovers just
above the pre-war co-op
all street noise buffered by wind
you're running late

142376
drone knows better
than to fly too close
to the sun
preferring to chart a course
through the city by the light
of your cellphone

N229RT
a young girl scatters
rose petals across the ground
before your approaching bride
drone lost among perfect
clouds and mountains
circles for another pass

EILEEN MYLES

NOTELL

It seems an unimaginable
Forest
I'm not talking to my
self I'm conducting
an extremely in
timate exchange with my
government
My brash smile
Means it's okay
Someone's dancing in
Clogs. It sounds
That way suctiony
I'm not here to con
Fuse the government
What I've
Got I share. The rubied surface of
Deteriorating cities moves me
To this. That is
what it's doing. I call
 It note. Note everyone getting
 Off here
I feel like being smart
As soon I seem stupid
I top it all up

I put on my cap.
There are machines all
Over the place. My friend
sat behind
The queen. Perfectly lucid
but Elizabeth
Kept going wtf she wouldn't
Shut up. Philip & Charles
Kept going
Mother.

BEN FAMA

CONSCRIPTS OF MODERNITY

empire. brand. persona. andré balazs (b. 1957) purchased the chateau marmont in 1990, at the start of a decade known as the longest period of peacetime economic expansion. personal incomes doubled from what they were during the recession in 1990. after the 1996 welfare reform act the united states experienced a reduction of poverty. the wall street stock exchange stayed over the 10,500 mark from 1999 to 2001. during this time, balazs expanded his hotel collection when he purchased and restored the mercer hotel in downtown new york, establishing "the benchmark by which other fashionable design hotels would come to be judged." the andré balazs luxury group's holdings now include chateau marmont in hollywood and sunset beach on shelter island. the standard hotels locations include hollywood, downtown la, miami beach, high line, meatpacking district and the newest addition, the standard, east village. in 2011, balazs launched a sea plane service to the hamptons, *StndAIR*, an 8 seat plane operating scheduled flights and charters from manhattan. this summer, andré balazs is pleased to release two new labels of his andré balazs collection of rosés. an international blend in collaboration with chateau minuty, located in the provence region of france, and a second, *sunset beach rosé*, being produced in partnership with the local winery on long island's east end. more a resort than cosmopolitan hotel, the sunset beach location includes a lively french beach-side restaurant and bar with sunset views and a luxury beach boutique. international hotel staff are on hand to assist in arranging all the local activities. do you like drinking wine?

if you can't afford it, affect it. known for its romantic small homes characterized by a low, broad frame building with end gables with a large central chimney, the cape cod house is synonymous with new england romance, designed to withstand the stormy, stark weather of the massachusetts coast, that thin curve of land in an endless black sea. during winter, darkness so wholly encapsulates "the cape," residents say it qualifies to have it's own time zone to account for the premature sunsets over the cape's drastically eastward bound longitude. its famous icy clear skies rendered into devastating sunsets. the cape and islands' regional suicide prevention coalition was formed in 2009 after statistics proved suspicions in cape cod were true: short days and long quiet dark nights correlated with high suicide rates. spring also appears notoriously delayed each year despite cape cod's high average of 200+ sunny days per year.

andrew sends me a warhol quote: warhol's asked "do you believe in emotions?" and responds "yes, unfortunately I have them." andrew has an extra ticket to paul mccarthy's *ws* show at the armory so i attend with him. it is july of 2013. 100 degrees. 21st century. later in the evening i cool off reading reviews of the show and wonder if a white man can ethically portray female exploitation and alterity, (meaning *could i?*) in the times review they relate the thematic content partly as determining nostalgia as a fool's faith. the times, in a separate but much longer article on frank ocean's rise to international fame, agree that maybe it is best for artists to give less when speaking publicly about their work. frank ocean's debut mixtape *nostalgia, ultra* was released free despite being signed to island / def jam who delayed movement on a release during the first few years he was under contract. *nostalgia, ultra* apprehends the past as source material on which to graft emotions. the cover to *nostalgia, ultra*, designed by ocean himself, features a early 90's model bmw m3 in neon orange, parked at the hedge of a forest. channel orange, his follow up album, for which he was paid a million dollars in advance, exhibits a pure swatch of the same orange tone.

these pure, 'natural' colors express instinctual life and threaten inwardness. look around inside a *bed bath and beyond* some time: gray, garnet, mauve, beige. reassuring certitudes for the anxious subject. in this regard bright color becomes apprehended on products as a sign of emancipation - often compensating in the home for the absence of more fundamental qualities (particularly a lack of space). the preserve® bpa free pasta strainer in "ripe tomato" or "apple green." cuisineart® dutch ovens in "provencal blue" "island spice red" or "pumpkin." having once represented something approaching a liberation, both have now become signs that are merely traps, raising the banner of freedom but delivering none to direct experience.

bpa, a man-made synthetic compound found in certain plastics, introduced into the mainstream by bayer and general electric in the 1950's, found now in products such as 99c disposable water bottles and other temporary food storage containers, has been reported to affect neurological functions and behavior. to avoid bpa, you'll want to avoid number 7 plastics, which as containers leach bpa as they break down over time, heat up in in the microwave, or are subject to hot water during cleaning. one way to avoid bpa is to use a stainless steel water bottle (like the klean kanteens carried right here at bed bath and beyond). and now on shelves are klean kanteen's new advanced design sport cap 2.0, which has a loop, dust cover and sport top. very convenient, very klean and very cute (see?).

kate moss saint tropez no tan lines. the huffington post reported that individuals engaging in bdsm sex suffer less anxiety and greater well being than others. july emotional heat index. diamonds fur coat champagne. totally gorgeous sunsets. netflix under the drone of the box fans. air conditioners reportedly in peak use on weekdays at 6pm. watching television online and wondering if my fashion has become normative and cinematic. when you start by imagining what it might be like, you step back, you think. how it makes someone feel. the experience of the product. this is what matters. this is it.

it's the year of the snake, and an elegant dress, bag, or shoe is one of the easiest ways to incorporate it into your wardrobe. an alluring pit of python sheath dresses and clutches is on the market right now. wearing just one serpentine element makes for a memorable look. click through for examples of this stunning trend, picks for pre-fall, the latest in berlin street style, beauty, people, parties, culture. spears first performed "i'm a slave 4 u" publicly at the 2001 mtv video music awards at the metropolitan opera house in new york city on september 6, 2001. along with dancing in a very revealing outfit, the performance is probably most remembered for featuring a number of exotic animals, including a white tiger and a live albino burmese python on her shoulders, the latter of which has become one of spears' most iconic images. the inclusion of the animals in the performance brought a great deal of criticism from animal rights organization people for the ethical treatment of animals (peta). in august 2008, mtv network named the performance the most memorable moment in vma history.

i wake up at 4:30 a.m. i never really sleep much and often start my day at this time. when i am very lucky and sleep through the night, i might get up at 7:00, but that is rare. the first thing i do when i get out of bed is weigh myself. i do this every morning, and if i have gained more than two or three pounds, i try to eat fruit and vegetables exclusively for a couple of days until my weight is back to my ideal. i make myself a tall glass of iced espresso (i don't like warm drinks), get into a hot bath, and slowly sip my drink as i come to life.

if you can't live off your wage, consider living at work. more than 20 percent of new yorkers may be living in poverty, the country may be on the verge of another war in the middle east, but this year's fashion week is turning out to be a weeklong party for the ages, with so many events, hardly anyone can keep them straight. remember the chris dorner manhunt? remember shape-ups? remember jay-z at pace gallery? remember the beginning of the recession of the american economy? people asked *would new york city be affected?* no, they'd say, it's too much of an international city.

the night before the first day in the office—well my mind just goes constantly—i took a sleeping pill, and had a dream that was really vivid. i was walking into my office for the first time. it seemed no one was there, it was possibly a saturday and my desk was near the very back of the floor. it was quiet, the floors were vacuumed, everything was untouched. the halls continued for quite some time. the serenity of it had a pristine purity. i thought *you know, i feel like i've been here before.* far back there was the glow of a desk lamp, in an office that look liked it might be mine. i turned and followed the path. within an hour i came into the office and there was an individual slumped back in the desk chair—myself—like i had been there thousands of years.

i think about chelsea as i am falling asleep. today i decide she's become allegorical of nearly 100 years of failed western culture, and in fact, likely the most important story and person of the postmodern era. born the second child of a squarely nuclear family, her father traveled while her british mother, who didn't drive, spent her days drinking. after their divorce, chelsea relocated to wales, where she became the target of bullying for being american and, living as a boy, for being viewed as effeminate. her mother's decaying mental health lead chelsea back to the united states to live with her father in oklahoma city, where she had violent confrontations with her stepmother over her troubled employment status. chelsea left for tulsa in a truck given to her by her father, sleeping in it at first, then moving in with a high school friend, whom she briefly worked with in a themed all-you-can-eat pizza buffet called *incredible pizza.* she soon after settled in with an aunt in potomac, maryland, for a 15 month period of stability while working, leisurely attending school, and dating. she enlisted in the military in 2007 with plans to attend college through the g.i. bill. she told her army supervisor later that she had also hoped joining a masculine environment would resolve her gender identity. trapped beneath the totalizing censorship of don't-ask-don't tell, and opposed to the kind of war in which she found herself involved, in january 2010 she began posting on facebook that she felt hopeless and alone. subject to solitary confinement after arrest, denied pardon after conviction, chelsea had the perfectly uncomplicated goal of "revealing the true nature of 21st century asymmetric warfare." coming out as transgender tazed the nation's media, unable to mature themselves to the contemporary politics of identification, most media outlets continuing to use the "he" despite the perfectly clear "i am chelsea manning, i am female" declaration. never on her own terms. sweet child from oklahoma.

court ordered chemical castration became legislation in 2033. cyproterone acetate was combined with an anti-psychotic medication; sex offenders had wrist sleeves procedurally implanted which deposited the hormone inhibiting serum directly into the bloodstream via reverse iontophoresis processes. lack of funding for prisons lead to shorter sentencing, but the convicted wore sleeves for life. everything was tracked. airlines merged into a symbolic oligarchy of parent companies. borders locked in cold wars fought over the last remaining fossil fuels. civilian travel applications lolled around bureaucratic networks. the rich traveled through a privately administered network of jets. the poor went unmonitored. international markets governed the wealthy. in 2043 the death penalty became nationalized under the flag. those sentenced were hauled to one of four national zones on the 1st of each month. contractors streamed the executions. scotus passed the 'treason act' and journalism became extinct. encrypted news traveled through torrents, a moving target for the administration. in a macabre act of political theatre, suri cruise, operating out of a digital commune of leftists, dropouts, artists and hackers, founded the 'funeral party.' under their platform, suicides among siblings and kin were encouraged by a proposed series of income tax waivers among their survivors. the families of euthanized elders collected payouts and substantial debt relief. amounts were determined by an age gradient. in time, cruise's gesture quietly became right wing legislature under the staid auspice of the "family care and protection act." the middle class rose from the grave.

continuously reconstituted through the things i desire. because i want things and need to be desired. when they say 'we're being authentic,' they mean 'we're extremely on message.' a content warning. a user history. i understand and wish to continue. i'm going in late to work today. and i'll probably be coming home late. love you so sorry, dear. a tax form. a loan application. the eighteenth brumaire of louis bonaparte. may be monitored. viva la vida. a whitening treatment. become a friend and save 30% today. shop the entire store.

ROBERT PINSKY

CLOUD OF MEXICO PORK

Too easy to laugh at the list of *trigger words*
In the *Analyst's Security Binder* as revealed
By a *Freedom of Information Act* lawsuit.

A website smirks at *Mexico* & *Pork* & *Cloud*
Amid *Al Quaeda (all spellings)*, *Hazmat*,
Enriched, Interstate, Nitrate and *Phishing.*

Delicious, unkosher, dark, vague, the Cloud
Of Mexico Pork threatens our borders.
Experts will improve the list, the logarithms,

Adapting meanings to effective analysis beyond
Effective and *affective. Adopt* and *adapt.*
Surveillance—French for *watching over*—

Preceded the apprehension of who became
The Disappeared. Their infant children, adopted
Were raised by *Intelligence Officers* as their own.

If I were *Experimental*, I would make
A poem consisting entirely of that list.
Random, Shale. Repurposed, Information.

JENNIFER KRONOVET

THE FUTURE OF WRITING IN ENGLISH

I

After being released from a concentration camp and becoming an exile in Shanghai, Charles K. Bliss invented a language of no sounds. A writing system of symbols to circumvent speech, its manipulations. Ideographic. Ideo. Idea. Ideal as the space between mind and page as silent.

In the future, English writing more and more becomes the opposite of this. Each word must be said aloud before it appears on the screen. Seeing, without saying—that's the manipulation. From voice, which has become content the way sex is the subtext. The flesh of meaning.

English adopts a notational system of dots and dashes above and between words to approximate tone, to make the speaking silently talk. We can't trust them, the words, to be the mind behind. A dot. A dash. The speech within speech.

II

In 2013, a Canadian company released the program ToneCheck that screens emails for potentially conflict causing language. Post-meeting anger: alert. Late night reach/bite toward a lost lover: don't.

In Future English, the thread of feeling in each word has become an overt overture, a prioritized primal focal point. Words are color-coded according to an emotional template based on the smallest fluctuations of pulse and temperature in the tips of fingers. What do we encode into words with our bodies as we speak? There is technology for this. It's right there in red red red.

III

Dear A,

I just want to say. I have been. I think about. Now you know.

With a feeling,

Jenny

TRANSCRIPT CONVENTIONS

⌈   overlap begins
⌊

  She can talk and listen simultaneously. Rain inserted into the river.

⌉   overlap ends
⌋

  He stops to hear. Self+other=negativeself now.
  The not-him of her talking pushes the side of his
  idea. The right-now mossy side.

=   links different parts of one speaker's continuous utterance when
     there is intervening speech by another speaker

  His speech, after she stops, continues on the same
  trajectory except with three new gravities: apple,
  her, rope. Its arc is the same without ever being an
  arc. Speech into speech—dye into skin.

–   self-interruption, halting, or stammering

  The self is stuffed into oneself. And then there is
  feeling. It all comes out, sometimes, as nothing.
  And three ideas at once. Is he still listening? What
  happens to them when she is trying to speak?
  They are further apart and closer as he guesses
  what she's about to say. And her idea becomes the one
  spectral representation. Paper stuck to a tree by wind.

...   a section or sentences has been left out of the transcript

> I'll admit it. I've used them for their words. What's
> missing: the words one forgets one even said.
> That's what I want you believe. The dust of speech. The
> microcosm of that dust.

(0.0) timed pause

> Once you start counting the pauses in people's
> speech... You fall in. I mean I. In the pauses—
> autobiography.

(.)   untimed pause, less that .5 seconds

> What can live in there? It just passed again. It was a
> memory of an animal moving. An unloved animal.

:   sound extension (the more, the longer the extension)

> Sound can mean the whole word again if she keeps her
> breath going through it. Wind through the flag saying
> *country* over and over. When the word finally ends—
> its opposite. The opposite of *country* is where you live
> then.

.hhh audible inhale (the more h's, the longer the inhale)

> Everyone needs to breathe. Sometimes emphatically.
> This inhale is elderly yet her. She tastes her future in that air.

hhh   audible exhale (the more h's, the longer the exhale)

> So rude—she knows—to fill space before his speech
> with extra breath. Like the flame in the hot air
> balloon—her wanting to lift it away.

.   stopping fall in tone

> Something died inside that sentence.

?   rising inflection

> But maybe not a question? But maybe you should let
> her know if you agree. The sky deciding to be one kind
> of weather for once.

!   animated tone

> She's talking about the new idea framing her. She and
> the frame are moving making the language skid. Tread
> marks.

↑   marked rise in intonation on the word that follows

> This arrow is a metaphor itself. The word rises, points.
> She just talks that way, she thinks. The words are
> always pointing.

↓   marked fall in intonation on the word that follows

> She dropped that one. He'll have to pick it up by
> leaning in. Then, it comes back to them as
> more. Exposed striations in the rock.

ABC increased volume

> Perhaps he didn't hear what she said.

°abc° encloses speech at a decreased volume

> Perhaps she didn't want to have to say it.

<u>underline</u> emphasis

> She stands behind some phrases as if she's pushing them forward with her body. She can't trust the language to move without her extra force. The flag articulates the air.

>abc<   encloses speech at a faster rate

> There's not much time left.

(abc) encloses a description

> (Then weather: sudden rain opening the ground to dark. The conversation moves inside.)

JORIE GRAHAM

HONEYCOMB

Ode to Prism. Aria. Untitled. I wait. I wait have you found me yet. Here at my screen,
can you make me
out? Make me out. All other exits have been sealed. See me or we will both vanish.
We need emblematic subjectivities. Need targeted acquiescence. Time zones. This is
the order of the day. To be visited secretly. To be circled and cancelled. I cover my
face. Total war: why am I still so invisible to you. No passport needed. If you look in,
the mirror chokes you off. No exit try again. Build bonfire. Light up screen. What are
you eating there. Can you survive on light. What is your theory of transmission. The
center holds, it holds, don't worry about that. These talkings here are not truths.
They are needs. They are purchases and invoices. They are not what shattered the
silence. Not revolutions clocks navigational tools. Have beginnings and ends.
Therefore not true. Have sign-offs. I set out again now with a new missive. Feel this:
my broken seduction. My tiny visit to the other. Busy. Temporary. In the screen
there is sea. Your fiberoptic cables line its floor. Entire. Ghost juice. The sea now
does not emit sound. It carries eternity as information. All its long floor. Clothed as
I am →in circumstance →see cell-depth →sound its atom →you need to look into here
further →past the grains of light →the remains of the ships →starlight →what cannot
go or come back →what has mass and does not traverse distance →is all here →look
here. Near the screen there are roses. Outside a new daymoon.

Can you see my room. Inside my room. Inside me where there is room

for what I miss. I am missing all of it. It is all invisible to me. Is it invisible

to you. You have the names of my friends my markers my markets my late night

queries. Re chemo re the travel pass re where to send the photo the side effects the

distinguishing features—bot says hide—*where*—bot does not know, bot

knows, what is it to *know* here, can you hear the steps approaching, I hold my

breath here—can you hear that—bot must also hold its breath—now the steps

continue past, we can breathe freely once again, in this hiding place the visible

world, among shapes and spoken words in here with my traces →can you please track me I do not feel safe →find the nearest flesh to my flesh →find the nearest rain, also passion → surveil this void →the smell of these stalks and the moisture they are drawing up →in order not to die

                                  too fast. The die is cast. The smell of geography is here: what is the smell of chain—invisible chain—the stone on my desk I brought back from Crete, the milk I did not finish in this cup. There is smoke from the debris my neighbor burns. Don't forget to log-in my exile. This one. Female MRN 3912412. I offer myself up. For you to see. Can you not see? Why do you only see these deeds. There is a page on my desk in which first love is taking place, there is a

page on my desk in which first love is taking place again—neither the characters yet knows they are in love—a few inches from there Mrs Ramsay speaks again—she always speaks—and Lilly Briscoe moves the salt—the sky passes by rounding us— the houses have their occupants—some have women locked-in deep—see them— someone has left them in the dark—he stands next to the fridge and drinks his beer—he turns the volume up so no one hears—that is the republic—are you surveilling—we would not want you to miss the women kicked in order to abort the rape—those screams—make sure you bank them you will need them—to prove who you were when they ask—I am eating—can you taste this—it is nut butter and a mockingbird just cut short a song to fly—I tap this screen with my fork—I dream a little dream in which the fork is king—a fly lands on the screen because it is summer afternoon—locusts start up—the river here are you keeping track—I know you can see the purchases, but who is it purchasing meàcan you please track that →I want to know how much I am worth →riverpebbles how many count them exact number →and the bees that did return to the hive today →those which did not lose their way →and exactly what neural path the neurotoxin took →please track disorientation →count death →each death →very small →see it from there →count it and store →I am the temporary →but there is also the permanent →have you looked to it →for now

THEY LIVE

There you are again.

On a site for a boutique in Maine, in your peach-colored luxe cotton slub tank top, "a perfect layering piece," you try to lure me, feline, a tad squinty, defiant.

You seem familiar even then, with your cleft chin, your blond hair loosely pulled up, your lips parted just so. All studiedly carefree.

I'm searching for a specific item, keep on browsing.

Next you train your come-hither eyes on me when I look up *eidetic* in the online edition of the Merriam Webster.

My memory is far from photographic and—face it—you're rather vanilla, but I recognize you.

You take another go at it on Travelocity.

On the Weather Channel you tempt me with a secret code. Free shipping with my purchase, a click away.

When you pop up on my Facebook page flirty turns pathetic. You're desperate, hardly becoming.

You're more than a headshot and your mouth is not hush.

I trick you into tracking me over to YouTube so we can watch Cookie Monster clips, a scene or two from a Carpenter horror flick.

Very meta, you sleaze.

EJ KOH

CLEARANCE

I browsed CIA.gov
for jobs:

> Targeting Officer,
> Intelligence Collection Analyst,
> Counterterrorism Methodologist,
> Librarian.

Be prepared to undergo a thorough investigation...

They found:

> I watched more porn than most women.

> I wrestled and, upon demanding
> an opponent two weight classes up, was
> publicly humiliated.

> I drank a cup of holy water at a wedding.

> I cannot hold my bladder past two hours, making me
> uneasy in the following places:
> > Subways. Banks. Bars, liquor stores. Boats.
> > Elevators, parks, outdoor malls, small offices,
> > beaches, buses, and waiting room. Funerals.

> I lied about speaking French.

"How to disable a bomb" in my Google search history.

I pass international customs with suitcases full
of red meat, greens, and seeds into the country.

No drug use in the past two years.

My elementary teacher asked why I'd try for the spelling bee,
and what the biggest word I knew was. I said, *masturbation*.
She sent me home with a red card.

I lie to people older than me,
tell the truth to younger people.

A Davis high school baseball team bullied me,
flipping my chair and making squinty eyes.
I tried to choke one of them
and was removed from class.

I laugh at racist jokes.

I feel responsible for the death of my two parakeets
and my grandmother.

I never litter.

I was fifteen when a Korean hairstylist proposed to me
inside a McDonald's in Tokyo, Japan.

I danced for a Hip Hop team for two years
by whom I felt largely betrayed.

My mother worked a shopping mall cart and fainted
when a customer stole a sixty-dollar makeup kit.

I believe in God.

The CIA called, I
passed.

MY COUNTRY

I want to be immortal. Not as a star
but as an ego.

The universe is female. Walk me through the story
of a mother dreaming of a pearl and a tiger

when she is pregnant. She does not tremble.
She is a mountain stuffed with people.

Frenetic lure in proportion to a meteorite
in the desert that will turn into a lake

the color of finger lime. I look out at the continent
where a gorilla named Michael

knew sign language and described what it was like
to watch poachers kill his mother.

TIM SEIBLES

FOR ALL

You watch
a starling's
timid quest:
a simple

life   afraid only
of the immediate—cars,
cats—having no
reason

to doubt
what it needs, no
lack of faith

in this clear day,
and no notion

of who's
behind the window
with so much

curiosity. For all

it knows, you are
simply the light

feathering its
small head, but

you wonder
what's inside

the bird, what
makes it fly: what
harmless

instruments
might tell you how
starlings think, why

they don't
see the Future

nesting everywhere
with sharp, hungry eyes.

DAMION SEARLS

SURVEYOR

All of the questions in Henry David Thoreau's The Journal: 1837–1861
(NYRB, 2009), pp. 77-97, in order

Do I not impregnate and intermix the flowers, produce rare and finer varieties by transferring my eyes from one to another?

If by patience, if by watching, I can secure one new ray of light, can feel myself elevated for an instant upon Pisgah, the world which was dead prose to me become living and divine, shall I not watch ever? shall I not be a watchman henceforth? If by watching a whole year on the city's walls I may obtain a communication from heaven, shall I not do well to shut up my shop and turn a watchman? We are surrounded by a rich and fertile mystery. May we not probe it, pry into it, employ ourselves about it, a little? To devote your life to the discovery of the divinity in nature or to the eating of oysters, would they not be attended with very different results?

One of the powder-mill buildings in Concord?

Was it the small rough sunflower which I saw this morning at the brook near Lee's Bridge?

Did I see privet in the swamp at the Bedford stone near Giles's house?

Shall we not add a tenth Muse to the immortal Nine?

What can be handsomer for a picture than our river scenery now?
Fell in with a man whose breath smelled of spirit which he had drunk.
How could I but feel that it was his own spirit that I smelt?

What can be uglier than a country occupied by grovelling, coarse, and low-lived men? No scenery will redeem it. What can be more beautiful than any scenery inhabited by heroes?

What is the autumnal tint of the black ash?

To have found the Indian gouges and tasted sweet acorns,—is it not enough for one afternoon?

Next I sailed over the sea in a small vessel such as the Northmen used, as it were to the Bay of Fundy, and thence overland I sailed, still over the shallows about the sources of rivers toward the deeper *channel* of a stream which emptied into the Gulf beyond,—the Miramichi, was it?

What have been the intimations of the night? I ask. How have you passed the night?

For the most part only the pines and oaks (white?) retain their leaves.

Ah, but is not this a glorious time for your deep inward fires? And will not your green hickory and white oak burn clear in this frosty air?

What is the use of going to see people whom yet you never see, and who never see you?

What more fit than that the advent of a new man into a family should acquire for it, and transmit to his posterity, a new patronymic? What is the churchyard but a graveyard?

Plenty of ripe checkerberries now. Do they blossom again in the spring?[1]

---

[1] Only once.

JOHN KINSELLA

NUPTIAL FLIGHT

It's Flying Ant Day at Jam Tree Gully.
An early spring, if that's what we can call it now.
We've already well and truly been sprung.
The virgin queens are guided from their bunkers
onto hillock runways, tended by their vested interests
in indirect and distant and over-familiar ways
(also the males with wings and exploding-genitalia-
in-waiting); the bright day flights begin with a flurry.
Launches are spectacular and we all watch, not even slightly
voyeur in the sheer wonder of colonial thanatos and birth-
of-nation stuff. The frenzy of an often busy empire
is the highpoint of history and ritual and belief,
this, too, is spirituality and sublimity on collision
course — and intervention is reaching into periphery
to lift the straying caterpillar frantically segmenting
across the priesthood and temples to Artemis, out of the dark
tunnels they come — it's too intense to focus, even to be
swarm — out of Hecate's chambers into 'conditions are right'
glibness of human watchfulness, curiosity and fear.
All marriages end in death, and our marriage night
is always to come, or lived over, or quietly recounted.
The breaking of the moon's meniscus in the glory of the sun.
Day and night becoming one, blinding by the light,
wing-glinting-rip into air, into the layers of kin.

SEALED IN / BLOCKED OUT

The last drop zone, last hole lost to the corner
of an old built-in wardrobe: free-falling mice
with no way back. No death-defying. No complete
annihilation of gravity. A fright night for young Tim
as they forced their way in, all other entries
finally tracked and sealed. And now this portal
blocked with steel wool and plaster. Each night
we sit and listen to the scurrying and fretting
at old entries: behind the stove, around laundry
pipes, behind cupboards. They work in teams,
in shifts, but don't break through. But there
are vague, diminished spaces where thought
is lost to anxiety: around window frames, points
where glass doors slide over glass walls, soft-
points where gyprock might be gnawed open.
But for five mornings now, the humane traps
have remained empty. The neurotoxic waft
of peppermint oil is fading with a hot breeze
that still finds entry points too thin, too small
even for mice. Sealed in, we've almost blocked
the world out — world that would come rushing,
forcing a way through dreams and brief silences.
How far into our heads have the mice burrowed?
Do we carry them inside out with us, everywhere?
Black-shouldered kites are in the ascendant
and watch us closely: hovering over paddocks,
any place mice would merge into the open.
We know that prey and pray are not homophones,
but precisely the same word. Things that sound
alike are one and the same: the silence of a diving

and a falling kite, the heart excited and terrified:
awaiting the small feet running over the ceiling,
expectation of an entry missed, a new incursion.
Or a weakness imagined, detected and made good.

RICHARD GREENFIELD

THIS UNDER GLASS STRUCTURE

I have seen the black triangular bird glinting behind the sun, the black balloon budding out of a cloud, I have tasted the black in the water— of sensors. Early in the millennium the spookbox on the wet wall in the abasement wanted its anonymous onyx to be leaked, to tell of the gyre of the web and the remorseless listening ear scanning its keywords. Not god, not idiot savant, but box. Breath equaled equation there, tinging the cosmos until dozens of new leaves erupted into the air from the twin black branches of a sidewalk tree, the antennae of this thing, and the grounding of this thing a flaring ant mound filled with transistors and meanness. For the record, I feel the gag order today, I spoke of and for the box and I spoke of and for the ineluctable body faceless, I cannot help but be organic about it... box and body seminally emerged into the lambent screen of the world with the burden of their yammer and erect disclosures... for the greater goodness... *Who need be afraid of the merge?* For it is the actual creation, a brief unclasped flower triggering, updating.

FOR THE QUANTITATIVE SELF SHALL SING AND TELL OF ITS HOLDINGS TO THE BOX
AND WHAT IT ASSUME IT SHALL ASSUME

WIRE TAP THERAPY

Redacted, fleshed abstract into a green field— the blacked-out pell-mell space in which one is victim but decoding upward into a sublime (cloudless) tenderpink (raw meat), shown-for-the-first-time (hymen) imperative (*you* is the subject of any imperative sentence) to wield violence (swing bat). In all of the tapes, you mention "blue"

(what is *that*?)

choking you for years, the ochre blue, the veiny fatherly blue, beaten blue in the sedge. In this attached image, a fat infrastructure proctors your throat, unhelpful to the analyst. Listen to yourself. Are you even alive to this pain? All former orphans of collateral damage only point to exhausted landscapes not reported to the secret court, but know

IT WILL NEVER HAPPEN AGAIN UNTIL IT DOES

JEAN VALENTINE

COULD IT BE HEAT?

Could it be heat? Could I be growing out? You my father
in a chair pulled up to the foot of my bed,
rubbing and rubbing my feet, under the blanket,

when I was eleven, when you came back from the war,
Sorry, you said, I can't speak, it's,
I'm dead. You rubbed my feet, a hundred years went by,

You sent me away to the library for love.
I found two books: the Window and the Door.
All I did was wait & sleep & write. Please change. Please open.

Another hundred years,
the Window opened me.
The Door said, More.

JOSHUA MARIE WILKINSON

HOW TO GET HOME IN A HURRY

Each way home
wanted its words

forming
a window

through song
except that it hid us

from findings
cold in the fields

atop new fiery
loams glistening

in the quake
stamping at wind

although I stood
unclothed calling

the birds off
without the force

of my larynx
crushed till

nobody listed
nobody yet

tried to get even
with the light

DANA ROESER

THE FIRE ACADEMY

I want to be a student
        at the Fire Academy
and not, as in
        my dream last
night, the gassing
        one. Why
did we all sit there,
        obediently,
in our detachable
        desks, new carpet
smell, gas seeping
        in, in that
sunken classroom,
        instead of fleeing?
It wasn't until the
        very end that
it occurred
        to me to not
wait for permission,
        to go. To gather
up the high school students
        in the "gathering
area" and whatever
        we were, teachers
in training—some
        version of
grad students. One woman
        had already

escaped. She heard the
        lecture, she saw
the list, and she
        said, Excuse me,
uh, I just have to
        go do something.

Blue spruce.
        Like a flash
of fire. Very tall. I forgot
        to look the
one time I was
        there since
25 years
        ago, at the
side yard. There was
        so much
to look at, my childhood
        house. Inhabited
by a music professor—and
        his wife and
the yipping schnauzers. He
        let me in! (His
wife wasn't
        home!) He
let me into the
        "elevator game"
hallway back
        behind the
kitchen, with its
        five doors.
But not upstairs.
        Dreams take
place all around
        there, even near

the split rail
        fence (surely
that's gone) near
        the spruce. A
display of
        Christmas trees.
We got them
        from the tree farm
each year with a
        ball of dirt. Do they
never die?

        Here, there's a spruce
tree back
        behind an
abandoned
        furniture
store—or is it not
        abandoned?
I can't quite remember.
        I know more than
half the retail "spaces"
        in that mall
are empty—
        and there
are cracks and
        exuberant
bursts of weed in
        the parking
lots. Not universally. Just
        in places. My favorite
is when a drive
        has been built,
a feeder
        road to some

prospective
        business, a "pain
clinic," a medical
        supply store,
an advance-on-your-
        tax-return-
loan-shark place,
        paved, organized,
curved and then
        just stopped,
cut off with
        a knife after
five or twenty
        feet. Nix
that project!
        I saw the fir
tree, I mean the
        spruce,
on a little slope
        leading down to
a small ravine, cattails,
        a slope up the
other side, separated by a
        chicken wire
fence leading to
        nothing, leading
to nature, trees.
        I was in
the "loading area,"
        orange back
doors
        for the mall
stores. One
        lonely car. Affair?
Drug deal?

Loading something?
The spruce
          was flaming
though. Thriving. Screaming
          of Christmases
past. I don't think,
          though, that some
child and her
          father brought
it out there
          one
holiday-aftermath,
          in its ball
of dirt.

          The Fire
          Academy is
the place for me. High
          school kids
in the country,
          in lieu of
"cosmetology" school,
          the Lafayette
Beauty Academy,
          are training
at the Fire Academy.
          And here
they can practice
          on real fires,
as the crews are
          all volunteer
anyway. (If fire doesn't
          suit them, they
can become
          EMTs.)

Where was
          it I lived
that there was
          a special
fire building
          on the
outskirts
          of town, off
of some four-lane
          semi-main-
drag? Many of
          the places
I have lived
          have been
flyover standouts.
          A four-
or five-story brick building
          sitting alone
by the road
          in some weeds. Used
for staging
          fires, death,
and destruction
          over and
over, and the fire
          students would
scramble
          up and down
the faces the
          staircases
looking for
          dummies, who
were posing
          as smoke-stricken
people or bodies.

I used
to look at that
place. Death
and destruction
headquarters.
Please let me
not state
the obvious: "If
only it could
be restricted to
that, to that
one building." The woman
escaped, with
a phony excuse,
a lie. Shall I start
with that? All the lies
I hear all the time,
every day. There are
so many lies
in the air, so much
willful
obfuscation, cheating,
why bother
looking for
the breathable
air? As a child, I loved
people half-heartedly,
already with a
shield. Only
person in the
security tent
was me. In the Fire
Academy all
of that is
burned off. You may

not be able
        to be heard,
but at least
        what interactions
you have
        can be trusted
to be genuine.
        Save me.
Save him. Save her.
        Get the
child. Get the cat.
        Crawl on your
belly under the
        smoke. I can't
breathe. I love
        you. I'm sorry.
Something's
        strobing
me, stroking me,
        basting me,
some awful
        clean thing
that'll strop
        me like
a razor, right
        against
my skin.

BEN MIROV

OBEDIENCE

What is your [master]
doing—I don't know.
I'm not privy—Is your

[master] making war—
I don't know. I'm not
privy—Maybe he is

making [money]—
My [master] does
not need [money]—

What does your
[master] need—My
[master] needs

obedience—What does
your [master] do
with obedience—

I don't know.
I'm not privy—

DANNIEL SCHOONEBEEK

FIFTEEN ANSWERS OF THE KING TO HIS QUESTIONERS

Yes I tasted my wife taste   the go-devil

they lowered   from heaven & I saw

the white handkerchief   they hung down

from heaven to earth   & I surveillance'd

three barrels: one liquor   one oil, one milk

& heard the first whisper   *I boil to black*

& heard the black whisper   *I boil to milk*

& heard the last whisper   *the milk boils all*

by itself yes I watched   the old warlander

she was lording me   over her colt & a black

grouse was present   he was tearing out

grass by the roots   & weaving this grass

in his fetlocks   this young horse was neighing

Yes I tasted my wife taste   the liquored

lie down on her shit heap   taste the curs

come to sniff   at the womb in stockades

in the courtyards   I tasted the catholics

they begged   to kneel down for a century

& I saw the horse   they prophesied I'd leave

my wife for: she had four heads   & each one

was grazing on clover   but only one leg

to sustain her yes I tasted   my wife taste

a worry rock no   a warchest of pearls no

a merit badge   & I saw the pigtail of smoke

that shook them   from heaven to earth

& I saw the chow line   & the rich in the chow line

& deserters were   handing out paychecks

demerits, bonuses   false teeth or flour

Tell me where   is my bonus said the desert

& the sacks   were picked clean yes I tasted

my wife taste   these stones with beards

like the devil's   they rolled down from heaven

& goose-stepped   when they tasted the earth

& three women I loved   from my youth I saw

weaving daisychains   & smearing each other's

wrists, each other's chests   with raw honey

& crowning themselves   with their chains

& pressing to steady their prayer   their wrists

to the earth   & I saw many henchmen

with horseshoes for eyes   with god's veins

in their barrels   with shoes filled with salt

& this is the devil's workforce I said   & I put them to work

JOANNA I. KAMINSKI

STABLE

When I built the kingdom,
  it was good. Then the fire came.

  God promised he could make
something honest out of ash, so he shaped

a hand. All my life I have been afraid
  I'm being lied to. It's a natural feeling. The horses knew it

  when they scuttled in the flames
toward an exit I unlocked

and held half open.

MAUREEN N. MCLANE

BABYLON MIC CHECK

As if ears
were not ears but body

swimming through
a common sounded space

How they embrace
it the new ones with nothing

they fear
to lose   to occupy

the street is to meet
and assemble, greet and garble

what truncheoned man
would flatten straight out

O Babylon
yours was a beautiful tower

it was no god
struck it down

MICAH BATEMAN

TO THE LISTENING ETHER

Tell me whatever
You might hope to find out

On the verge of inventing telephones
Over a floor of soggy maps

The brick-and-mortar server system
Out of bricks, I limped

Shoreward under showering arrows
Having thought of Timothy as "not a threat"

Like a canary cast from a submarine
In our devices, no opiates

As a conspiracy theorist
Who couldn't think on his friends

With only the purest love?
Neither speech nor static

In the electromagnet's lee
Nothing transmits through a vacuum

But beneath whose land?
The struck-through lithography

Of border planets
We learned sooner than the age-old question

The formulation
Of the querying syntax

A Quaker? Or his hands trembling
In sync with the air

There is no "to hear"

JED RASULA

NERVOUS MUSIC

Out here under the neocolonial bigtop,
in the intersubjective padlock of fieldwork,
adjusting our headphones and chastity belts, the voice-over
in the prosthetic garden of eden of Harlequin fiction
forgot to mention the three little piggies
asking for "Heat Loss." But what if
"mere appearance" is the soliloquy of the Home Court Ad-
vantage Hypothesis? Expending strategic initiative
through vocal parasites in the private sector
isn't the only missing link up their sleeves.
Debtor nations' mental shotput
peeling the balloon of market ideology
without releasing the helium
is both a challenge, and an oper-
an oppopper,
an oppoppertoo,
an oppopertunity
an opera tune unity you micro-chip chums can't refuse.
To have bred a part of that story—his or hers—
that history urges our tail to swell, why it might be
anything, anything at all: if it's not sir or mister, it's
genetic etiquette, rounding up & judging
the world for the purposes of life,
noise for the purposes of nervous music. If it's not
one nation, under the odds, with justice invisible for awe,
it's bounty hunters & mousketeers
injecting fertility drugs
into their foreign-policy skits,

conspiring to power the payload into a deeper space.
Whenever the weapon itself delivers the arms
contract to the next of skin, you're talking
style.

Just in case you thought you'd ask,
now you know.

ANDREW DURBIN

PRISM

At dinner, Katy Perry cried into her napkin. "It's no big deal," she said, waving away her personal assistant, who retreated to the corner of the room. "It's really no big deal."

"Why are you crying?" her current boyfriend demanded, turning to her. He forced a smile at all of us around the table, his first and only gesture toward anyone else at dinner besides Katy. She looked away from him. I thought the current boyfriend should chill, but he repeated himself, putting his hand on her shoulder: "Why are you crying, *Katy*?"

She shook her head. "I'm fine, OK?"

"*Surrrrrrrre*," he said, lowering his head toward his plate. He poked at his Isle of Gigha halibut. "Whatever."

I looked at Katy, who stared blankly across the table, just past my shoulder toward the shadowy hallway that led to the kitchen. We were at a dinner hosted by [REDACTED], a well-known record producer who had recently terminated his contract with Virgin Records and moved back to the city where his parents had raised him, where he had attended Bronx Science, and where, in college, he had listened to Madonna's "Vogue" and decided he wanted to produce other people's sound. A wax candle separated Katy and me. It had been dripping onto a plate of white asparagus all night—the same ghostly color as the summer vegetable popular in New York that year—and was nearly gone. The room was dark and the apartment evoked—at the muted end of the Bloomberg administration, with its sleek, glassy high-rises—the sillier vibes of a haunted house, an older, vaudeville New York, gauzy with cobwebs. We could hardly see the food on our plates.

The producer's old Upper East Side flat had gone unchanged for sixty or so years, he had told us at the start of dinner. His parents died there and he "took over" shortly thereafter, among rumors of a breakdown in Aspen.

Katy wore what looked like several dead flamingos wrapped around her from ankle to Katy wore what looked like several dead flamingos wrapped around her from ankle to chin. The birds' necks had been twisted to form a high collar finished in gold thread and little tufts of green fur. She had described it to me as "romantic couture" when we took the elevator up to the apartment together. Perry is gorgeous by nonspecific design, accumulating color and fabric without ever fixing a permanent look, except perhaps vague kitsch, itself somewhat chic. I tried to find the heads of the flamingos among the pink feathers, but if it ever was a flock of birds those heads were long ago removed, thrown away in the garbage, the necks stuffed and sewn up, tied and fitted to form the collar of the dress.

Katy Perry had just released her third album, *Prism*. It was, at the time of our dinner, number one and showed no signs of slowing down.

[REDACTED] returned to talking about his friendship with the boys of One Direction. (We had been discussing, among many things, American vs. British pop.) We all leaned in, Katy too, as he recalled the time he swore he saw two of the boys, Louis and Harry, enter the same bedroom after a party in Tokyo, holding hands, even though the boys had been booked separate suites. When [REDACTED] asked a member of their security detail about "the sleeping situation" the next morning, he said Harry never left Louis' room. "They can't keep their hands off each other, you know."

"They aren't gay," I said, turning to the woman on my left, [REDACTED], who nodded in agreement. She was the dinner's resident expert on American politics, but she counted pop music among her exceptionally broad interests. Her father was a senator and she served as a representative in New York's delegation in the House. "There's no way," I said.

"Have you seen them in concert?" [REDACTED] said to me, "How they touch one another? So gay!" He was solemn and a few people mumbled in agreement. Representative [REDACTED] finished her glass of wine and shook her head in disagreement.

"No," I said. "You need more proof than that. They're just being boys."

"Boys, all right," [REDACTED] said.

We were all very drunk. Some people turned to Katy to search her face for any hint she might know about the love lives of Louis and Harry, but she had already assured us that she had no inside information (throughout the night she claimed she was too busy to have friends in the music industry). In any case, she didn't seem to be paying attention to anyone but her current boyfriend, who kept whispering in her ear in an excited, somewhat irritated manner. Finally she frowned and waved him away, then turned from all of us to stare at a wall, where somewhere her personal assistant must have been standing in the shadows. I hadn't thought the star of the night would fade so quickly, but by the second course she was nearly gone: quiet, indifferent, distracted. Her melancholy rendered her a barely visible blue at the edge of the table where the candlelight dropped off.

"The proof," [REDACTED] said, mostly slurring, "is in their entire team, which is not only composed of assistants, producers, and other handlers, but also: a corporate mass electronic surveillance data mining program—known in some circles as DARK HORSE—run by a shadowy group of privacy experts who work at great distance from their immediate circle but who keep close tabs on them, and a number of other important celebrities, in order to control and manipulate their private lives, creating an environment of paranoia that ensures they behave on-brand and according to certain market-friendly values. Whatever they do is what gets out; the music industry—Hollywood, too—learned long ago that, in addition to controlling the media and its 'narratives,' they had to control their product on the most basic level, that is, on the level of their personal lives, by essentially erasing that privacy and colonizing what remained. This control ultimately proves effective in terms of curbing certain off-brand impulses, like, say, gay sex among the boys of One Direction, by creating a restrictive, paranoid culture of information-sharing. Everyone lives in fear that their secrets will escape and alienate them from their fans, their source of income, and fame itself. Everyone knows that someone might know something, and so nothing changes."

He paused and made eye contact with me. I felt my jaw go slack.

Katy and the current boyfriend stood up. "We're leaving," she said. She turned to the current boyfriend: "Let's go."

"What? No," [REDACTED] shouted. He stood up, knocking over his glass of wine. A waiter hurried over with a cloth to wipe up the spill, but [REDACTED] pushed him out of the way. Katy and the current boyfriend exited the dining room, flamingo feathers peeling off as they rushed to the door. The personal assistant trailed behind them, texting the driver below to ready the car. (She kept yelling: "Texting the car, texting the car!") [REDACTED] followed them into the vestibule where they stood waiting for the elevator. Everyone at the table leapt up and moved to the hallway that led to the scene. I gathered the feathers in the dark as I moved toward the front of the apartment, where our host frantically was frantically pleading with Katy not to go. "I was just kidding," he said.

"No," said the current boyfriend. "This is *so* fucking ridiculous." Katy said nothing and didn't look at anyone. When the elevator arrived, she stepped into it and flashed us the middle finger.

"Fuck you," the current boyfriend said as the elevator doors closed.

Katy Perry's *Prism* begins parade-like with "Roar," soundtrack to his-torical remainders rediscovered on other shores, locked in the purple light of Audis on the beach or among south Florida palms on Ocean Drive, getting fucked up on the beach, getting like really fucked up on Five Hour Energy, recoiled in glassy rainbows rising out of the sea. Katy Perry makes me feel like I'm high in the mall or tripping on GHB in a public pool. Days rendered speechless with my hair full of sand, all this blonde hair full of sand and I can't stop: "Dancing through the fire cause I am the champion and you're going to hear me roar." Like really, I can't stop. It begins a thing flittering behind the system at present, idiotically beautiful in its neon glow, the revolutionary agent of a social life made to bloom at gunpoint into something-ness, dizzying, embers left of the Members Only jacket burned at the bonfire. It is endless and somewhere there is a phrase to describe it that will come to me. I suppose it's a ball. I suppose it could be something else, too. In *Prism*, everything is leveled by a pop indifferent to individuated life. Love is everywhere and nowhere at once. It renders the varieties of experience singular, sucking it all in: flattened, affectless, and blissed out like a night spent drinking on Venice Beach. Katy's music is a mutant pop, collating genre without ever assuming the pose of a stable P.O.V. Only "Dark Horse," which begins with a high-pitched "oh no" before it descends below the stadium benches at the high school football game to romance taken up among the shadows, Eros made cosmic in its troubled gorgeousness, suggests any configuration outside the usual boy-girl love, boy-girl breakup, boy-girl regret, boy-girl make-up. "Make me your Aphrodite, you're one and only. Make me your enemy," she sings. Later: Juicy J raps, "She eat your heart out like Jeffrey Dahmer"—a necrophiliac cannibal who murdered, dismembered, and consumed seventeen boys in the 1980s—before he reverts (as the album often does) to cliché: love is an addiction. But is Katy addicted to dismembering and eating her lovers? In her America, which closely resembles everyone else's, we love fuck party live forever, even if living forever happens to be terminally clichéd: "All we have is this moment," "They say one man's trash is another man's treasure." It is a feeling that organizes other feelings into one feeling that describes only itself: an ocean of nostalgia that I love to swim in.

The dinner party followed them down in the next elevator. When we arrived outside of the apartment, Katy stood on the sidewalk, waiting for her driver to pull up.

"Katy, Katy," [REDACTED] said. She looked at each of us, moving her eyes from face to face, but said nothing. Her current boyfriend moved forward to block our host from getting any closer.

"Hey man," he said, "I, like, really need you to step the fuck back."

"No, no, I understand," he said, "I just don't see why you have to leave. I am happy to apologize. I am *sorry*."

"Sorry won't cut it, asshole," Katy said. I stared at her neck in the streetlight to see if I could finally make out the heads of the flamingos wrapped into the collar, but I still couldn't see any of them. Our host tried to approach Katy and the current boyfriend, but the current boyfriend stepped up and pushed him back.

"Man, I told you to step back," he said.

From around the corner, a Bentley pulled up and stopped at the entrance to the building. A driver stepped out and opened the door for them. She frowned at us before entering the car. I watched her slide onto the red seats into the heavenly seclusion of its leather interior. The driver shut the door. [REDACTED] began to knock on the window. The driver immediately yanked him back by his shoulder. "Touch my car again, buddy, and I'll break your fucking hand."

"OK, OK," he said, and stepped back, putting his hands in his pockets.

The driver nodded and got into the car. They drove off.

Katy's sudden absence felt oceanic. But when I looked at it, at the vacant, shadowy 72nd Street, I saw nothing, neither the other dinner guests nor the car as it began to turn onto Lexington. I saw nothing that would allow me to define "ocean," as in the biological and ecological contingency that has come to mean "ocean," let alone "absence." This, like other things, was OK, even a little nice. *Prism* is itself an ocean of feeling. Its waves quiver under a moon the shape of Katy's transformative, prismatic face ebbing in the dark, haloed in blue.

Your ocean is flowing toward me, Katy, I thought, as I stood under the canopy of a palm tree at the empty shore, which wasn't so much a palm as it is a pun on the fist un-balled before a reader who began to trace its creases. He ran his fingers along the groove of my palm, searching the revelatory lines that have crossed one another to locate the coordinates of some future rapidly becoming present.

I asked him what it meant, but he just shook his head.

I looked at him and tried to understand what this might mean, but he didn't seem to know. He sat at his desk and sighed, looked at his computer screen, and transferred information he located in several databases into a few Excel spreadsheets open on his desktop in preparation for an extended memo due at the end of the week. His chair squeaked and he wrote a post-it note to remind himself to tell head of operations that he needs a new chair. He occasionally looked at the clock near his outgoing mailbox. As always, he felt "stretched thin."

He often wondered if his co-workers were as bored as he is. He doesn't have an office window to look out of but he frequently likes to pause in his day to imagine what is outside the building: the parking lot, the road that leads out of Virginia and back to D.C. He finds this life theoretically beautiful though in practice he could see himself doing other work. That other work remains unknown in its details to him but he thinks about what it could be fairly often. It would be some- thing practical but beautiful.

Whenever the song "Dark Horse" plays on his iPod Shuffle, the reader thinks about suggesting that title as a name for a program the office—or rather, the complex of agencies collated into what he refers to as "the office"—is developing. The song, like the other songs on the album, reminds the reader of a time he had dinner with a high school girlfriend's parents, the night of a significant local high school football game. Her father was an intolerant man who, after 9/11, found a vital resource for his hatred in the Internet. Her father peddled in conspiracies related to the complicity of the Bush Administration in designing and executing the attacks, which he cryptically referred to as "the Opening." He would often begin sentences: "Before the Opening" or "After the Opening." The Opening, as he described it to the reader, was the event that both admitted the veracity of the lie and the falsity of the truth simultaneously; that is, The Opening articulated two points about reality, holographic in its lush, simulated surfaces: one, that the perceivable conditions of life in the United States were lies that covered up the generators of those conditions and, two, the lies pre-empted what created them and so remain the primary "reality" (and not, as shadier conspiracies might have it, the reverse). He liked to say that facts were useless things. What matters is the dream that gives those facts a purpose, a life.

After that dinner, The Opening became a frequent reference point for the reader as he left his hometown, attended Georgetown University, and began to work in the D.C. metropolitan area. He often thought about its merits and debated it with himself privately. Soon the reader began to feel the Opening everywhere, at every instance, whether he was at work or at the gym or having a drink or listening to *Prism*, which he gradually discovered (as he discovered with many, many things) was based on this exact twinned-point. Perry puts it more simply, the reader thinks, in arguing that the fantasy that renders the present experiential does not conceal a "deeper," more "true" reality. Rather, it is fantasy that allows reality to spread.

He leaned back in his chair. It squeaked under his weight.

"Dark Horse" evokes the early Sunday hours at the height of the American weekend, the last minutes before sunrise, when you either choose among the dazed remnants of the night or go home alone. Also, the highly organized systems of information management that cache, tag, and categorize both the metadata of these remnants (text message: "hi what r u doing rite now its late i know"; recorded as "Message containing no flagged content sent at 3:02:42AM 11/08/13 from Maison O, 98 Kenmare Street, Manhattan, New York City, New York 10012) and the remnants themselves (recorded as: ANDREW SCOTT DURBIN, resident of 855 Park Place, Brooklyn, New York City, New York 11216; born 09/28/89; profile clear of flagged content. SEE MORE). The cover of Perry's *Prism* features a photograph of the artist taken by Ryan McGinley, whose work effaces the marks of aging and those that differentiate youthful bodies by reducing them to a blur, blotched in the sunlit fields or the caves out west, flakes of flesh tones in which only the vaguest outline of a thin college student emerges, naked, un-seduced by the camera itself but in love with the audience at the other end of the process that manufactures his image. People stare at them in the gallery or scrolling through a blog on their iPhone, the faces staring back, sometimes very clear, sometimes still blurrier, prismatic, triangulated as viewer, model, and the networks of distribution for which Ryan McGinley serves as a conduit for an idea of beauty not exactly universal as it strives toward a uniqueness defined by the unexpected intensity of the sight of someone's sharp pelvis or high cheek bones but getting there. They are strange, even ugly in McGinley's terrible photographs, and yet this doesn't deprive them of their magnetism. The three of us—model, Ryan, and me—begin to organize into a record of taste to be graphed by agencies more or less invisible to us. I text my friend "hi what r u doing rite now its late i know" and even though I am certain no response will come I go deep and send it again. The impulse is, itself, based on a belief in the dark horse: that a thing probably won't happen leads me to think that it must. In [REDACTED]'s apartment, everything darkened as we resumed our places at the table. In the candlelight, I stared at the cover of Katy's new album, narrowing in on the little A in Katy shaped like a triangle, a prism, over Ryan McGinley's sun-drenched image of her as she catches the light, and it became easy to see in it another prism, lying in repose among the sunflowers, the quartz pyramid through which light becomes a rainbow or in other iterations, rectangular or cubic or pentagonal or, finally, the hexagonal crystal, in which I see myself telling Katy to back up a step, please, Katy, can someone get her some make-up please? and raise the silvery cloth up to your lips before the green screen where my assistants later overlay the field that seems real but probably isn't, or back of that, another prism that spins in a nest of light, tagging content endlessly, storing that content into the plural databases where I take residence among the machines who read me, who render me legible in various other systems languages, flagging "bomb," for example, like, Katy Perry is the bomb, Katy, you're the bomb, as the prism spins in my hand and I bring it close to speak into it, pressing it to my lips, under a prismatic sunset a gradient of red like the stroked, reddish brown hair of a horse moving across a field, the field where the sunflowers do not wilt under the hand of Ryan McGinley's assistants, the horse moving quickly through it, running up and turning back at the electrified fence over and over again in a game it plays with the only environment it knows. I raise my phone to take a picture. I hold it close, tap the screen to focus the image, but the horse moves too quickly and I only manage to snap a photo of a blur. I post it to Instagram anyway, marking for friends and the servers mainlined to the various agencies that might take note that somewhere, I saw a horse, and that that horse was moving fast.

JESSICA BARAN

LIFE DURING WARTIME

Yeah, yeah, said the cab driver. The car TV said: see and be seen is more than a pedestrian slogan. What you want is watching you—the eye of a strange cartoon. Let's stack the multiples, the extra copies of our smaller tasks. There: a calendar year. A pile that has no sense of itself, no desire to look further. A torn out page from a chemistry textbook falling from a window and directing your line of sight from one neighbor's bedroom to another's porch. This is the new surveillance proposal: to sing you a song for you to sing along with. Sing it. I feel close to what I witness. I love an ocean breeze. I love to shut my eyes and be touched.

CATHY PARK HONG

INSIDE BEYONCÉ

My dad once walked in on my dream
    Don't you have any privacy settings
An old man was massaging my scalp in a bath
and it felt delicious, then Dad barged in
        Buy Pantene Rinse for
    I only have dreams of people streaming
    into my dreams

    Oh wait, that's Imogen
I've blocked her. Her traffic causes migraines.
    She's a megaplex of selfies
If she shat out scrabble tiles, she'd have better spelling
    No, it's Beyoncé, I've been waiting
    forever to gain access
Is she still alive

    Boring! Beyoncé's just thanking God
    and her ten thousand handlers
I don't think she's alive
    The more people you thank, the more you're worth
I have no one to thank. I'm worthless
    I wish I had a paywall to hide behind
I'd kill myself

I keep his carbon data in a locket
    Your headvoice is oily. It needs a rinse
His embalmed traffic is inside me
            Latest news on Pwanu Trafficking
    I hear they get exiled into their bodies
Gross, my lipids are now viral.

    Can you zoom in
I see human-trafficking ships over an ocean
of dead links, no, they're fish
    Your Dream Recall is epic
Then I realize I'm in one too but I don't care
    Is this an ad-free zone
since this old man's massaging me.

    This is my hometown
I'm giving you a tour of my reverie
    You're in *my* reverie
He used to tickle me with his knuckles, it hurt
    That's my *encrypted* memory
as if he didn't think I knew his thoughts,
but I knew, and he knew I knew
    Stop thinking what I'm thinking

that he loved me more than my sisters
    You're so full of envy, it's sad
    how you hack into me
which made me feel secretive and guilty
so I learned to train my thoughts into an
ever long performance
    because there's nothing inside you,
    you're just a plug.
But I have this pang.
    It's my pang.

DEPRESSION

Depression—it's a public feeling
But what if I don't like anything as much as I pretend to

Darling Darling Darling
What if I don't even like you

The blue night with trees
Everything told me to feel something

And yet everything you said was a lie
And all my emotions were for nothing

Oh all they want you to do is cry cry cry
Cry they say Cry

The animal takes the shape of the spirit
And the I is no I

Hardly on the girl
But why?

I had two main ideas
That I brought to the forefront

But the ideas never moved the audience
To laughter, to pick the pockets

So I tapped a little peacock
With the fiery tail

Until no one knew what was there

Sadness
It's a public feeling

So I cry and cry
And the silver moon goes shining

Thunder and lightning
Thunder and lightning

I woke up in mid-morning

And it was all chatter
Just thunder and lightning

GLOWING LOSER

Neon coming from outside me cursed be
Light from the most high I want you
Ditches in my head I fall in every dawn
The bad soldiers in there want me corpsed

I am sorry soldiers
Get on your knees and become women
Become my women
Worship light and in doing so transform

Do not ask me how
Something has to do it for you
Something higher or other
An inner other
A sky in there
The good sky

Fall on your swords
Don't die
Become other
See you as the sky sees you
See me that way too

HOA NGUYEN

JANUARY

January long light
Janus   I see you

2 faced looking in Capricorn
Capricious like the snowy owl
        irription

We fear heavy body collisions
God of doorways and gates

January   time of doors
time looking back on itself

    spelt and salt

They say when you walk
through a door

You can forget
    what you came for

BIRTHDAY POEM

Illuminated behind a skin
a grey   the sky with fat
fast slants of snow

Fire Horse poet   This is a birthday
poem   squeaky underfoot
the snow and Jeanine's cookies

I drive husbands and fathers
to early deaths   Push the knife
into the cake to cut it

Me the supposed bringer of ruin
(money)   Covered in fondant and
violet flowers

It's my birthday   My eyes are older

TOMAŽ ŠALAMUN

TO WHOM SQUIRTS BLOOD FROM HIS NOSE

Once I would like to talk calmly with Perčič
about Bud Hopkins. I'd love to report to him
what I saw. What does Bud do with my

friend SW, who's already the third generation
of the abducted. It started with his grandfather
who was US War Minister in the Second World War.

Besides the official program they were interested in
the pantry. They too have vacations, unions,
idlers, they too, in the remote galaxies, have a

statesman who throws the population on trains,
saying: Travel, we're rich enough, all to the sea!
Creatures eat sandwiches and look through the

windows. Bud has a young wife. He was a painter
first. We negotiate quietly. I show him my holes
from their nibs. Carola lives in the huge castle,

once in the countryside. Her buddhist clashed
with Bud. I believe him and I don't believe
him. In fact I don't believe him.

GRAHAM FOUST

VISAGES

Quietly at times, or else
as loudly as possible, existence
outwits its particulars.

For instance, my reflection's
defective—I'm reversed there,
permanently so,

and so never the "you"
whom everyone hides from me
without trying to—

but in photos, frozen
and in almost no mood,
I seem only a little alone.

STEPHEN BURT

DEAR DIGITAL CAMERA

Nathan told me when he was six,
to write a poem about the universe,
but I couldn't finish it. I had no place to stand, no place to see it from.

Yesterday he said, more hopefully,
that I ought to write a poem for his digital camera,
new to him, though six years old to us: lime-green, palm-sized—

though larger than Nathan's palm—and, at least today, inseparable
     from Nathan,
who runs, leaps, crouches under tables, ambles and spreads himself
     out on both floors of our place
 trying to find new angles for more pictures,

duplicative pictures, time-lapse pictures, dazzled blurred or pinpoint
     still life pictures, portraits, and stop-motion
animation, applied
to anything and everything.

Last week he kept pointing out
security cameras in grocery stores.
"Why are they spying on us?" he asked. But now

he spies on us: the milk cup not yet spilled
then spilled, the tumbler on its side,
on crumbs, on inescapable abstraction,

that is, extreme close-ups of window-glass and carpet—
all are his and therefore ours. They make
a sort of second universe,

which he can show me how to understand,
one that stands still while ours moves.
This morning he couldn't stop moving—he and Cooper

chased each other up and down and up and down and up and down
     the stairs
like weasels, like halves of a clinching argument,
about to prove a conjecture, or hit a wall…

He says that if I write a poem to his digital camera
he will then write back, in the camera's own voice.
It may be the voice of experience or of fear,

or of exuberance, or of thin air.
When you are a camera, nobody can see who you are;
you get to see them. You get to decide what they see.

Sometimes you'd rather not. Last night
he asked me to take a picture of himself
as he rammed himself into the frame of an IKEA chair—

he had done it once; he wanted to do it again.
He said I should press the silver bar halfway down,
to get it to focus, and then all the way down

to fit whatever was in the frame. The frame,
he continued, would hold for a millisecond
(his term); if he then ran towards me ,

he would be able to catch up and see himself
before he dissolved into grainy approximation,
like clouds seen through sieves, before they, and he, moved on.

EMILY ABENDROTH

REFLECTION #2: MUGSHOT MOVEMENTS
Excerpt from MICROFICHE / MICROFILCH /
MICROMANAGE / MICROFEIGN

While the presence and apparatuses of everyday surveillance have
unquestionably expanded in scope in our own moment (and in the
wake of the so-called Global War on Terror), these are neither entirely
new forms of state and corporate invasiveness nor unprecedented
efforts at resistance to those forms.

When precincts, courtrooms, wards, and prisons first started
taking "mugshots" of individuals for policing purposes, the state
of photographic technology was such that each print still required
a somewhat lengthy exposure time in order for the image to be
successfully and crisply captured.

Hence, a subject, who was alternately and energetically moving about,
left behind on each visual slide a negative imprint of
ghostly, indeterminate anatomical trails
        of multiple, flailing and semi-transparent,
            cross-contaminating body parts
        of facial cartwheels and the soft trickery
            of maverick lips

A tipping point
at which mobility could confer illegibility or, at a minimum,
                                a register of movement only.

And this identificatory loss of grip was something that could be worked to one's quick advantage if accurate inscription was not something that one was looking to voluntarily provide in the circumstances, at least certainly not in the idle guise of "proof" or "justification" for the forceful implementation of further constraints to one's being.

Instead, conceding to yield to authorities a suitable paper icon of oneself became a singular favor that one could physically refuse to bestow
> via the purportedly "ignoble" galvanization of exuberant thrashing
> via the elastic implementation of amplified brow and mouth contortions
> via the unrepentant tantrums of one's limbs – their nimble and kaleidoscopic spasms of gesture

> In reference to the persecuted, the definition
>> of discourteous
>>> is almost always equivalent to self-preserving.

To curve and buck the torso,
until what you became on film was something filmy, something
intrepid, orbital, blotched, abnegated

> to decline to hold one's head in "appropriate"
> "vagrant" alignment
> to play host to one disdainful cranial shit fit after
> another in order to insistently be blur
> to be smear, so as to avoid the perpetual smear
> campaigns that accompany penal classification

To remain unpersuaded by repeated enjoinments to graciously
> join the process of one's own adjudication

In response to such mendacious overtures on the part of the captured, the presiding overseers subsequently tried to elide any prospects of acrobatic technical sabotage through the use of such interventions as: the introduction of metal forceps to station the head; the gratuitous lending forth of leather straps and rigid iron clasps to master up preferred photographic postures; the clasping of a guard's hands around the animate neck of each and every detained person; the urgent, commanding "guide" from behind who requires of his subject a dejectedly compromised but upright demeanor.

The lord of the manor, and of the mannerism,
who mandates stillness for the sake of a criminalizing
likeness, regardless of whether the one so violently nested
in those cupped palms liked it or not...
                    likes it or not.

A hot war over representation fought before the untoward and cold
impatience of the camera lens
                    its well-penned and pinning documentations

A rogue composition whose subject was nonetheless still
capable of rejecting its frames

they stood ranged, arranged	*wide-wayed and strong-grieved in metal sleeves*
truncated to mere trunks in profile	*filed before a sinecure, a circular aperture*
a sure matter of record	*a muscular impression*
a bent joint, a joist cavity	*an all too moist exposure*

        Sometimes the gamest foil you need is your very own
           body in recoil
        Sometimes simply by whispering, an uncooperative
           or "soiled" voice
        Can go blissfully undetected by even the choicest
           of systems

NICK ADMUSSEN

CHARACTER STUDY WITH PHOTOMANIPULATION

Here is a photograph of two men
aboard together in the Moscow Canal;
here is an identical photograph
with just one, the commissar has vanished.

Commissar Yezhov exists in a quantum state.
Nikolai Yezhov is a cat in a box.
He leans over the boat rail next to Stalin
half-smiling, responsible for water transport
and also is gone. They called him the poisoned dwarf.
He never existed. His assistant
had him beaten before he died.

Clearly, the regularity but not total sameness
of the waves behind him proves that Stalin
stood alone on the ship. Nikolai Yezhov
arrested half the Soviet military. Nikolai
Yezhov's ashes were mixed with others'
and you'll never find him, now. He built
the execution chamber where he was shot
and said he'd die with Stalin's name on his lips.

Nothing was reported
or written. He sobbed and hiccuped.
The waves in the photograph where Nikolai
Yezhov is not are basically unruffled.

Here is a photograph of one man
in which you, also, do not appear—although you
do not command the secret police,
although you were not feted in the Bolshoi
in 1937, there is a probability that you are alive
and one that you are not, a Committee discusses you,
how to clean you, whether to instruct
your children to forget you.

Yezhov wrote that all opposition
inexorably ends in death. It does not matter
that you embrace the revolution. You feel loyal
but you are a traitor by nature, palming
small profit, a memory, some stolen days,
smirking into the camera with your tiny plans,
as the boat drifts downstream
towards the organs of your government.

MARK BIBBINS

WITNESS

1.
Religion happens after birds eat
berries and carry the seeds overseas
in their bellies, language gets
around on the condition that bees
drag it out of flowers. Punk and dub
had to travel in other vessels,
the latter made of space
and the former none or at least
too little. Songs are always built
and dismantled at the same time,
always demanding to see
pictures of themselves.

New York London Paris Munich
Munich Paris London New York
Paris Munich Paris Munich
London London New York New York

A few people are still alive, you'd
have heard them if they'd sung,
a few others too, if they'd
a sound among them to sing.
The eyes!
If history ever comes for them,
the eyes can hide in the mouth.

2.

abjectness abruptness absoluteness abstractness abstruseness accurateness acquisitiveness acuteness adroitness aggressiveness aimlessness airworthiness alertness allusiveness aloneness aloofness amateurishness animateness apprehensiveness appropriateness aptness arbitrariness archaicness arduousness artfulness articulateness artificialness assertiveness astuteness attentiveness attractiveness audaciousness augustness awareness awfulness awkwardness backwardness badness bagginess baldness balkiness bareness baroness baroqueness barrenness baseness bashfulness bitterness blackness blamelessness blandness blankness blasphemousness bleakness blessedness blindness bloatedness blueness bluntness boldness boorishness bounciness boundlessness boyishness brashness braveness brazenness briefness brightness briskness brittleness broadness brokenness brotherliness brownness bumptiousness burntness burstiness business callousness calmness candidness capaciousness capriciousness carefulness carelessness casualness cautiousness cavalierness ceaselessness ceremonialness charitableness chasteness cheapness cheerfulness cheeriness cheerlessness childishness chilliness chivalrousness chubbiness cleanliness cleanness clearness cleverness closeness cloudiness clumsiness coarseness cockiness cohesiveness coldness combativeness comeliness commercialness commonness compactness competitiveness completeness conciseness concreteness conduciveness connectedness consciousness contagiousness contemporariness contrariness coolness copiousness correctness covetousness coziness craftiness craziness creativeness credulousness creepiness crispness crudeness currentness curtness cuteness cutesiness daintiness dampness dangerousness darkness deaconess deadliness deadness deafness dearness deceitfulness decisiveness defensiveness definiteness deliberateness denseness destructiveness devoutness dimness dinginess directness dirtiness discreteness disingenuousness disinterestedness disjointness distinctiveness distinctness divisiveness dizziness doggedness drawnness dreariness drowsiness drunkenness dubiousness dullness dumbness duskiness dutifulness eagerness earliness earnestness earthliness easiness edginess effectiveness effortlessness elaborateness electricalness elusiveness emptiness endlessness enormousness enviousness erroneousness evenhandedness evenness exactness excessiveness excitedness exclusiveness expertness explicitness expressiveness exquisiteness extraneousness extraordinariness eye████████ faintness fairness faithfulness faithlessness falseness familiarness fanciness fastness fatness fearlessness feebleness ferociousness fewness fickleness fierceness filthiness fineness finiteness firmness fitness fixedness flatness fleetness flimsiness floridness floweriness fondness foolishness forcefulness foreverness forgetfulness forgiveness forthrightness forwardness foulness frankness freeness freshness fretfulness friendliness frightfulness fruitfulness fullness funniness furtiveness fuzziness gameness gaudiness gauntness gayness generousness gentleness genuineness ghastliness giddiness gingerliness gladness glassiness goldenness goodness governess gracefulness graciousness grandness gratefulness gratuitousness graveness grayness greatness greediness greenness grimness grossness grubbiness guiltiness habitualness hairiness handedness handiness handsomeness haphazardness haplessness happiness hardheadedness hardheartedness hardiness hardness harebrainedness harmfulness harmlessness harmoniousness harness harshness hastiness hatefulness haughtiness haziness headstrongness healthfulness healthiness heartbrokenness heartiness heartsickness heaviness heedlessness helpfulness helplessness heterogeneousness hideousness highness hoariness hoarseness holiness hollowness homelessness homesickness homogeneousness honorableness hopefulness hopelessness horribleness hotheadedness hotness hugeness humaneness humanness humbleness humorousness huskiness iciness idleness illness illustriousness imperviousness implicitness impressiveness inadequateness inappropriateness inclusiveness incompleteness inconsiderateness incorrectness indebtedness indecisiveness indefiniteness indigenousness industriousness ineffectiveness inertness infiniteness ingeniousness innocuousness inquisitiveness insidiousness instantaneousness intentness intrusiveness inventiveness inwardness irateness jauntiness jealousness jerkiness joblessness joyousness justness keenness kindness lameness languidness largeness lateness lawlessness laziness leanness levelness lewdness lifelessness lightness likeliness likeness limpness lioness literalness littleness liveliness liveness Loch Ness loftiness loneliness looseness loudness lousiness loveliness lowness ludicrousness lusciousness lustiness madness maleness maliciousness manageableness marvelousness meagerness meaningfulness meaninglessness meanness meekness mellowness melodiousness memorableness mercenariness meritoriousness messiness methodicalness mightiness mildness milkiness mindfulness minuteness miscellaneousness mischievousness miserableness mistiness moderateness modernness moistness momentariness momentousness monotonousness moodiness morbidness motionlessness mournfulness muddiness mustiness mutableness muteness mysteriousness naiveness nakedness narrowness nastiness naturalness naughtiness nearness neatness needlessness nervousness newness niceness niggardliness nimbleness nobleness noisiness nonbusiness nosiness nothingness numbness obliqueness obliviousness obviousness oddness odiousness odorousness offensiveness officiousness oldness ominousness oneness opaqueness openness oppositeness orderliness ordinariness outspokenness paleness passiveness pastness patroness peacefulness perfectness permissiveness persuasiveness pervasiveness pettiness physicalness picturesqueness pinkness pithiness plainness plaintiveness playfulness pleasantness plumpness poisonousness politeness pompousness poorness populousness positiveness possessiveness powerfulness powerlessness precariousness preciousness precipitateness preciseness preparedness presentness presumptuousness pretentiousness prettiness primeness primitiveness promptness proneness properness protectiveness punctiliousness quaintness qualifiedness qualmishness quarrelsomeness queasiness queerness questionableness quickness quietness quirkiness raciness raggedness rancorousness randomness rankness rareness rashness rawness readiness realness reasonableness rebelliousness recentness receptiveness recklessness reddishness redness reflexiveness relativeness relentlessness reliableness religiousness remarkableness remoteness repetitiveness repleteness representativeness resistiveness resoluteness resourcefulness respectfulness responsibleness

responsiveness restfulness restiveness restlessness restrictiveness
retentiveness richness ridiculousness righteousness rightfulness
rightness ripeness riskiness roadworthiness robustness roominess
rosiness rottenness roughness roundedness roundness rowdiness
ruddiness rudeness ruggedness ruthlessness sacredness sadness
safeness saltiness sameness savageness scantiness scarceness
secretiveness selfishness selflessness senselessness sensitiveness
separateness seriousness sexiness shadiness shakiness shallowness
shapelessness sharpness sheepishness shiftiness shininess shortness
shortsightedness shrewdness shrillness shyness sickness silliness
simpleness sinfulness singleness skillfulness slackness sleepiness
sleeplessness slightness slipperiness sloppiness slovenliness slowness
sluggishness slyness smallness smartness smoothness smugness
sneakiness snugness soberness softness solemnness solidness
solitariness sordidness soreness soundness sourness spareness
sparseness speechlessness spiciness spiritedness spitefulness
springiness squareness starkness statuesqueness statutoriness
steadfastness steadiness steepness sternness stickiness stiffness
stillness stinginess storminess stoutness straightforwardness
straightness strangeness strictness stringiness stubbornness sturdiness
stylishness subtleness succinctness suddenness suggestiveness
suitableness sulkiness sullenness suppleness sureness surfaceness
surliness sweetness swiftness talkativeness tallness tameness tardiness
tartness tastefulness tastiness tautness tediousness temperateness
tenderness tenseness thankfulness thanklessness thickness
thoroughness thoughtfulness thoughtlessness tidiness tightness
timelessness timeliness timidness tininess tinniness tiredness
tirelessness tiresomeness togetherness touchiness toughness
transitiveness treacherousness trickiness trimness trustfulness
trustworthiness truthfulness typicalness ugliness unaccountableness
unadaptableness unadaptedness unaffectedness unawareness
uncleanness unconformableness unconsciousness uneasiness
unevenness unfairness unfaithfulness unfitness unfriendliness
ungratefulness unhappiness uniqueness unkindness unlikeness
unnaturalness unpleasantness unreasonableness unselfishness

unsteadiness untidiness untruthfulness unwieldiness unwillingness unworthiness uprightness usefulness uselessness vagueness validness variableness vastness verticalness viciousness vileness villainousness vindictiveness vividness wantonness wariness wastefulness watchfulness weakness weariness weatherproofness weightlessness weirdness wellness wetness whiteness wholeness wholesomeness wickedness wilderness wildness wiliness willingness wimpiness wiriness wistfulness ██████ wonderfulness woodenness wordiness worldliness worthiness worthlessness worthwhileness wretchedness wryness yellowness youthfulness zealousness

NIKKI GIOVANNI

SURVEILLANCE

Who was there...who looked
Where was the camera
That Saturday night my father
Hit my mother so hard
She literally flew
Across the living room
And fell against the window pane

Like a rag doll

Or a wind up toy
That a child is tired of playing with

My sister has gone out
As she has friends...I suppose... and places
To Go

I watched
I watched over Mommy
I hear her say to him
Please don't hit me
But he does

She says to me
What goes on
In our house
Stays
In our house

I am a camera
I am the silent film
It was recorded because
I surveilled

I hid out
In my bedroom
With a flashlight ring
That let me read

Until it was time

Who saw what I heard
Who knows how to make sense of it

And we want to save the world?

What about my mother

I am a witness

I don't need an overseas enemy

I have a father...

And the band played on

DARA WIER

REVERSE SURVEILLANCE

It isn't so much that you do it, it's how you do it
and that you do it on purpose
while pretending you're not doing anything.
It's not so much that you spy on me it's that your intention
has always been to erase me.
It's always been difficult
to understand how your knowledge of me
increases my invisibility.
The more you see me the less I'm there.
The solvent you use isn't apprehending so much as it is
eliminating,
not so much affirmative and loving as it is
dissolving and dismissive.
Especially your tactic that involves how you say
I never existed.
As if the more you know about me the less
there is.
Our relationship is a lot like a worst-case scenario
romance. Ending excruciatingly unbearably criminal
for one of us.

AUTONOMY IS FREE

Ironed elegies, no risk,
Like a red moon
Over this brown desk.

Deep down,
You are made of tears,
But why repeat it?

Or, would you prefer
A honeymoon's daylight
On a theory of barking?

Have another one.
Suburb of cats,
The medals that we win

Are "nomadic."
Under pressure,
It is like this most times.

The onanistic comma,
Midnight stretched out,
The way people jostle

And shift
While the friends move on.
Keep it clean:

What has passed at
Some midpoint
Has simply fallen away,

And you, little one,
Notice things
In a star's essence:

Blond hair of the
Thief
Returning to his crime.

WE

We cross over an age's anarchic gyre, we
Get emotional. We blink. What are you
Trying to prove sidewalk? Devoid of the me
That has warned you in bright lights, without

A trace of plausible explanation, we go
Together, take a very hot bath. Without you,
I am a bundle of sensations. Oxygen,
Overalls, this pair of rubber boots. We are

Now in the refrigerator, getting warmer
With our breath. Listen, you just could not
Go any further with the me, valiant comrade
To this stillness that passes. I don't want to

"Grow" anymore. I just want to sit here
And bathe in our light that blinds, and sing
Songs about rivers or stars. Plump as a
Lamb, the universe, you and I, in it.

KENT SHAW

HOW THE DATABASE IS POWERING THE NEW WORLD ECONOMY

No one looked at us and thought, now there go a couple good-looking lists,
even when we had plenty of lists written out at home, that we kept on
      our desk, and in our email.
Sometimes we posted detailed lists along the hallway, and that's what
      led to the kitchen.
Lists about us.
Lists about thriftiness and pecan pies and surprises and vocabularies
      and shapes,
totally innocuous shapes, and Winston-Salem. We really liked
      Winston-Salem.
We had long lists, and lists of very long things, that had many
      different segments.
And that made the list very confusing.
There were lists about us. I said that.
And then another list we were forever trying to keep open.

Like the list of Modernisms I was keeping in secret for my
      significant other.
She's a very private person,
and keeping a list of Modernisms is kind of like keeping a list
      about privacy.
Or maybe a Modernism is quiet enough at night that you can think a
      lot about yourself,
and for most people that feels like a list.

In the world of computers, you use a database to keep track of
      these things.
One of those three-dimensional objects they call a database engine.
A list of lists that goes on into some kind of ad infinitum.
It's like a government with a government inside it listing people
      I liked, then deleted,
then held up in limbo so that they feel like they're in some Modernism
that's blocked in by a dumpster.
And there's a graffiti on the side in that wide script graffiti makes, and
      it says, "Take that."
Yeah, take that.

The other night I had a dream. The dream was a mountain.
with all the dimensions available to a mountain, including a full
      mineral inventory,
cubic allotment of resources, density measurements
and, of course, a cave for birds, at least the birds that could support
      the life of a mountain.
The problem is a dream should not have its own inventory.
It could have a personality. Or a plan of action.
It could be a mountain.
And a mountain should be darkness. Animate dark and
      inanimate darkness.

PAUL MULDOON

RITA DUFFY: WATCHTOWER 2

1

From here it looks as if the whole country is spread under a
   camouflage tarp

rolled out by successive British garrisons

stationed in Crossmaglen. As teenagers we worked our way
   through *Iosagan*

 Agus Sgealta Eile while selling shocks and struts

from a tumbledown garage. Our vision of Four Green Fields shrinks to
   the olive drab

the Brits throw over everything. This must be their version of a *tour
   d'horizon*,

their scanners scanning our hillsides while we still try to scan

a verse by Padraig Pearse. One advantage of a farm that, as they say,
   bestrides

the border is how industrial diesel

dyed with a green dye ferries itself from the South into the North

by force of gravity alone. The fact that laundered diesel's then worth twice at much at the pump supports the usual

tendencies of the punters to misjudge

our motives and see us as common criminals. Like seeing smoke in a
   paint smudge.

2

One of our neighbors, interned for selling *An Phoblacht*, learned we're
   not the first tribe

to have been put down or the first to have risen

against our oppressors. That's why we've always sided with the Redskin

and the Palestinian. It must be because steroids

are legal in the North but not the South the Brits like to eavesdrop

on our comings and goings. As for kerosene,

the fact that it's cheaper in the North is enough to sicken

our happiness. That and the upstarts

who try to horn in on our operation. We're in a constant tussle

with these Seoinins-come-lately, a constant back and forth

on the business of smuggling fuel. We run it through cat litter or
   fuller's earth

to absolve it of the dye. By far the biggest hassle

is trying to get rid of the green sludge

left over from the process. It infiltrates our clothes. It's impossible
   to budge.

JONI WALLACE

I AM OPPENHEIMER

The film goes silent. The canyon lit by tracers,
petal smoke, a Braille of "loves me, loves me not."

No dossier, save that scrawled
into dust on the cadillac, "Wash Me."

Which photographs worth taking?
Equations etched into headstones.

Red shift, blue. Animalcules.
Sky impromptus, mare's tail formations

silvering juniper, a silver-gray mare.
I place myself there, quicksilver.

Mr. Los Alamos. Mr. Manhattan.
Mr. Mole. Blind illusory game,

see how it spires, spent-fuse, a million
chalked cities, my eyes-no-longer.

DAVID CLEWELL

WHAT IF ALL ALONG WE'VE BEEN WRONG ABOUT TINFOIL HATS

(i.)

and they're not quite everything they've been cracked up to be,
so instead of rendering the wearer impervious
to government-sanctioned mind manipulation or any other
mental interference whatsoever—thereby allowing us to keep
our thoughts and only our thoughts to ourselves, under
our control alone, inviolable and whole—these hats in fact
are amplifying certain signals from the outside, making tinfoil more
or less the unofficial headwear of state-supported confusion,
and we who have been so conscientious, so downright vigilant,
wake up one day to discover our station as hapless government dupes
or worse, the unwitting pawns of our alien overlords on Earth
paving the way for an invasion guaranteed to meet with absolutely
no resistance at all, thanks to these hats that enhance the power
of whoever wants inside our heads to get there without fail,

these hats that were supposed to protect us by repelling every manner
of radio frequencies, microwaves, electrical impulses that might otherwise
alter chemicals in the brain, reconfigure the hard-wiring already
jerrybuilt at best—these hats can't even fend off late-night-radio
    talk shows,
TV evangelists, ABBA songs, those pitches from personal-injury lawyers,
or the ceaseless chatter of once-distant relatives suddenly in our
    living rooms,

so what chance did we have against professional electromagnetic
    distortion
or hypno-assassination programming, Manchurian-Candidate-style,
or someone imprinting the latest version of the New World Order agenda,
let alone the incessant national elevator music piped in to insure
a softened-up population, grown somehow more docile than ever.

ii

At the height of the Cold War, government spooks were all over
this idea of *Electromagnetic Hearing*—headgear that would *facilitate
covert message reception* for people they knew to be on our side
but also might *function as a nonlethal weapon of disruption
by inducing voices in the enemy's head,* as if said enemy really could
be talked into wearing so ridiculous a thing in the first place.
In those exhilarating years of nearly giddy R-&-D,
it was never about keeping any voices out. They were looking for surefire
ways to sneak the voices farther *in.* And so they spread the disinformative
opposite word entirely—*a reliable defensive posture*—then sat back
and waited for the tinfoil hats to start showing up in the streets: tinfoil
beanies, tinfoil fedoras, tinfoil hunting caps with tinfoil earflaps—genuine
American ingenuity at work, no matter how profoundly misguided.

But my Uncle Bud, whose middle name was usually Misguided Ingenuity,
wasn't falling for the hats. This was a man forever extending
the reach of his ancient TV's wobbling rabbit-ears with tinfoil—
his very own precarious Super-Antenna. His one and only
    Herculean labor.
He suspected such hats would make matters much worse—
    they were nothing
but indiscriminate receivers wide open to a world full of trouble—
and Bud was a man who surely knew his way around a roll of foil.
He insisted we'd be better off just putting our fingers in our ears,
closing our eyes, and singing at the top of our lungs in the dark again,

drowning out voices we'd rather not hear with a favorite TV-show
	theme song
over and over. He was partial to *The Flintstones* because it seemed
	to promise
that if we choose more carefully the company we keep, there might be
brighter days ahead: *a yabba-dabba-doo time* could yet possibly be had,
but *a dabba-doo time* at the very least.

iii.

But if you're still attached to the idea of a hat, consider a material
more innocuous than tinfoil. Maybe you could fold yourself an
	old-fashioned
newspaper hat—something you never before saw the point of,
	really, even
in kindergarten. No tough guy, no hero, no self-respecting
	neighborhood kid
could afford to be caught dead in such a flimsy get-up, but then again,
you always knew what you were getting into. When you put on a hat
like that, there weren't any crazy expectations. So why not go ahead
and fashion a cardboard sword while you're at it? There's bound to be
someone who will actually believe that you're not afraid to use it, either.

And if it should rain, yes, you'll be waterlogged, completely soaked
to the skin, but where's the serious harm in that? Chances are you'll live
to fight another day. A tinfoil hat's a different story altogether, the
	last thing
you need in rough weather. It tends to call the lightning down. Better
	to be
a make-believe sailor or pirate who's managed to ride out one more
	storm—
good news anyone can see for themselves in the ink running down
	your face.

And no one's about to tell you anything you haven't already thought of on your own—even if you can't always seem to remember exactly what gave you that idea to begin with.

ELISA GABBERT

FROM *L'HEURE BLEUE*

At the poetry reading,
I scribble in a notebook.

The girl with the bee tattoo on her back
satisfies my need for "luminous detail."

Dusk falls. *L'heure bleue.* Black trees
silhouetted over indigo sky
is my favorite sight,

a streetlight unfurling
its liquid red beam.

I maintain a certain level
of detachment like a buzz.

A man makes eye contact.

There are times when desire seems
to transfer. He communicates desire;
I am infected by desire.

It's the worst kind of desire—
too thin a film
between desire and reality.

Jack always feels like someone is watching.
So we turn it into a game.
We do things for their benefit.

We invent a code name for suicide,
"The Attractive Option,"
and refer to it often.

Emerson said, *For every minute you are angry
you lose sixty seconds of happiness.*
But he also said, *the purpose of life
is not to be happy.* I say to Jack,
Life makes it impossible
not to waste your life.

Speech is a charade, of course,
but sometimes I think things
for their benefit. An idea
is part of the persona.

I'm interested in the point
where the game crosses over,
where he is laughing
and I am afraid.

I don't fantasize about sex,
just kissing him. Somehow,
I don't embody me. I watch it
in the third person.

It's like looking in a mirror,
but we're out of sync.
I don't want her to see me.

Jack asked, *Why do you just lie there?*
I hadn't noticed. When he was here,
I found him a distraction.

My hands feel gigantic
in the dark. I touch every edge
of the bed.

D.A. POWELL

MAKING LIKE MONKS

from *The Voyeur's Guide to Real Estate*: Now, voyeur—I can see you,
    too. I am the angel of perception. I am the angle.

Be cool when you're talking round the fuzz. "I'll have the cheeseplate,"
    as if they don't know what that is. They know the lingo.

How many times have they heard, "I'll give you a dollar if you spit on
    it." They know the boy on mushrooms. They know the tango.

You're passing out. And we've just met! Now, like a tuft of carpet,
    we've been carried to the streets. Through the bay window.
We can see the delivery boy from the Thai place is hiding something.
    Maybe he's dropping off the *pad see ew*, if you feel me.
Maybe he has handled those noodles like a brief romance. There is a
    code to the open window. It appears we've run out of space.

AMY KING

I GO GUNSLINGER

When I say "My soul's a leather apron," I mean everything
I shouldn't.

That you should cleave the meat of me for your sacred cows,
clean off the bone with chemicals of any other name
than Sarin gas or U.S. American Grade A ground chuck.

That you dress for them in Army fatigues and put on the apron
of legitimacy, and your scars. Oh your scars are bar talk for bedding
     women later.

I too bed women, and smile for the mirror smiling at my gay proposal
     dockside
upon ship's return. Look what rights I've won for the limited!

My leather soul is akin to a mask for when I walk the streets filling
     hollowness.

I pull it tighter, stretching skin, and ask, "What would you have me do
     for this side
of Country?"

I wrap it, Gunslinger, and do not ask the savage mind for a Levi-
     Strauss pass.

The Oxycodone delivers a pleasant dizziness from which to throw
        lopsided stones
under ground cover, and eat the eyes that would have me
        for breakfast.
Love's tracheotomy uncovers
nothing, and I let the fly live
that would undo me with its nothingness.
I earn so much gay marriage of import.

Drugs too are a source of nature just as killing is a source
        of nourishment.
I am paid by the highest order a tepid sum to ride on. First world income.

Don't get me wrong; I'm not suggesting you abuse or sell nature
in dime bags. That would be a horrible instrument of humanity
to persist on. Let me do it for you, from poverty and minority-lacks-
        potential status.
I've been sold onward.

To keep you safe, I see everything through the lens of orders. Just
        give that shit to me
and move along. You have no direct power here.

When I blast the shell across my infrared panopticon, just know that
the collarbone exploding in another city-not-your-own
is limitless. It goes on for miles and will greet us down the road as
        ashen stardust
upon the meat of our tables.

That collarbone is a lovely tragic arc, traceable only by tongue to palate,
best consumed as salt upon our steaks in the dimly candlelit
        romantic dark.
Open mouth, insert prison.

Rise and repeat:
I am the blood, the bread, the light.
Swallowing leather is a form of inebriation, if you can stomach the
    wine's origins.

I absolve you of everything now, which is what I meant in the beginning.

THE STARS ARE CALLING, SKIN SACKS

See, your chemical warfare is no warfare I
Bend over the altar, shove
My tongue into your daylight, finger
Your escape routes,
the riffs and struts
On wireless maps, a participle medley from your breathing apparatus
Singing the Body Technology, a schizophrenia always giving back.

The way they watched me felt like love,
I said let me write you like love,
Let me write you like love's fire.

But I missed the star guts crashing the Global Market ways,
Crushing me with its gentleman hands, eyes without a face.

Every man is a symbol
Along the axis of Rorschach etchings.
I see your face again, the fluorescent light
repeating my face back to me. Echo chamber,
I learn so much in hiding, my electric nest cake.
Google-maps for the brains attached.

In Real Life sexual dimensions hold it against us,
Could not map us out of eleven dimensions.
They would just go on forever, smudging the details down,
wearing us the fuck, most pleasantly, out.

JOYELLE MCSWEENEY

SWAT CYCLE

Why would you wound upon wound up a
starpastied widow jet
black wig o'er a pale pink
sweater set heat rises sweat pastes the bang
to your powdered breast the jet sets the chain
of pearls to 'swing' like a lampchain
slots back and resets tac light on a fair brow strung up
at the fair ground safety off on a tear on a
virgin wi(n)dow flight tests the vice
waiting in the john to be sworn in holds up
the flight with his knees holds up a
finger for the check two fingers for a
nother round forty rounds at the
mall hopeless marble ballustrades will
catch ordnance better than a brow bone cleaves and
self-grieves the cops scoop the tills clean brain matter like
kitty litter litters the scene the scene's pristine
of cash the jet set
lifts
    off
        carves a doggy contrail now on air as air
goes greezey where the
wheezy sound dam goes collapse copside
on tarmac all bellies sigh
o'er gunbelts the dogrun
's encrusted in
what god wants
little bits of aerated

prayer nozzle pater noster toothed ring
trained on your red
crosshairs
chevalier medallion for your neck

*

genuflect
before the idk gross grotto the polaroid in
Ridyah jacquard loom pomegranate preprograms
the future slots for
furniture ads star carnivals nude treif nylons tiara circus act
     the rusting
highnotes the two-toned vocabulotic sclerotic siren
     steam-engine
spine veronicas the sweaty cheek of the sky, its stray hair, its
     discomposed air hostess
sash air marshalls the secret star on its chest
star of morning O Dis
combobulated coronal goes round and round like a donk
Balthasar following the fraud light
right out of Joachim Du Bellay sways a swagger and surely a
happy belly bellowing grumpy gallows gassing uh cashing in a
lowslung island check-cashing chain where those
heavy hoofbeats sunqe in mud and made a marque on the ranck
     parquet
the lady loudspeaker clumps up on struts:
corkney orkney islanders offshore bankers come in
     answer code
the onleyst castle like a gas mirage
furtive merkin buncker gak gag order goggle moat
-el et inverted castle constellated rotating cast roasty-roost
et sulkey soot-encrusted caboose
soundbooth oubliette essoess skinz ornithologisyllogism no birdz

[Keats] the red light means
ON AIR sleeping on the luggage carousel
at Louis Armstrong Internationelle first world would wormwood
        where a sybilline
teen raises a wrist in the bridge light to clock the time
the current jumps the spiney
knock-knocks the cops
freak the comments field the
spunky oilfield gives jet to first
thirsttooth
edema patina edible pantie line chocolate gun cabinet crap shoot
Psalms
in the snifter
of the mind:

> in the crossed struts of the struncture
> in the black golt in His goiture
> in majescule in slim black margins type
> speculum in blister O let down your lettery blood type
> O junk bail bond lay me down in payday
> dawn O maglite a sky swept clean of starts
> drop a clout cover a cleaver a clover loan
> in camera down the sewer a remote
> controlled port a truncheon a nightstick a baton a
> crowd management device a spray
> of buckshott or of pepper to the eye O this bridge strut's a site
> of embarkment to the moon tonite punch
> my punch card tie my ankle up ignite

RAE ARMANTROUT

EXCHANGE

City of the future
in which each subway station's stairs
lead to the ground floor
of a casino/
mall.

*

What counts
is the role
defined for each piece
by a system of rules saying
how it can move,
not the stuff
the piece is made of.

*

In the intersection,
a muscular, shirtless man
with small American
flags tied to each wrist—
so that he looks
like a wrestler—
pushes, no, shoves
then catches, a stroller
piled high with plastic bags —
his stuff.

*

City of the future,
where a tramway to the top
of a peak
opens onto
a wax museum
in which
Michael Jackson
extends one gloved hand

APPROXIMATE

Wait, I haven't found
the right word yet.

Poem means
homeostasis.

"Is as"

As is

Film is enough
like death.

In a bright light
at the far end,
attractive strangers gesture.

They are searching
the system
for systemic threats.

I was going
to pay attention.

Attention passes
through a long cord

into the past
progressive

RAPHAEL RUBINSTEIN

POEM BEGUN ON A TRAIN

Excuse me while I adjust the privacy settings of this poem
so that if it's ever published it will exist as a legible text
and not as a string of stubborn phrases I silently repeat to myself.
Three lines written, now three and a half, yet for the moment no one
but me has access to them, as they stretch haltingly
across the perfect grid of my Rhodia notebook,
unless, that is, Amtrak has installed
hidden video cameras above the seats in the coach class
of this Northeast Regional and one of them is focused on this very page.

Whoa, that idea came a little too easily.
The belief that your every move is being watched
used to be a sign of clinical paranoia,
except for those living under totalitarian regimes
in which case it was a perfectly reasonable assumption.
Now it's becoming a perfectly reasonable assumption
no matter where you breathe, no matter where you write.

Let's assume that Amtrak hasn't installed
individual video surveillance, at least not yet.
Let's further assume that this poem, which is slowly crawling from
        pure potentiality
to an intermediate state of being more concrete
than if I wrote it by fingertip on a steamy window
but less so than the station signs howling past,
has no other reader but me.
Still, once I transcribe my handwritten draft into my MacBook Pro,
a nearly inevitable step I am already contemplating

and will have long since accomplished by the time you read these lines
it will have become so easily available to endless numbers
of bureaucrats and hackers that I might as well post
the whole thing online immediately.

Every poet thinks about every line being read by someone else
even if, as the line is written, its author suspects that he or she may die
before those words will win the attention of any other human being.
Positing a reader, sympathetic or dismissive,
is apparently necessary for every poem,
from the most compressed, tongue-entangled lyric
to stanzas as aerated and matter-of-fact as these.
There are times, however, when a reader is not merely posited
but becomes as factually undeniable as the poem itself.
What's more, instead of turning a cold shoulder
or bestowing ceremonial kisses on a prize-winner's cheeks,
this invisible reader rattles a set of prison keys
and is ready to dispatch an inconvenient text and author
to a cold library with zero opening hours
from which nothing circulates except ashes.
To earn shelf space in this grim depository
a poem doesn't even need to be written down.
Think of Mandelstam's "Stalin Epigram,"
16 lines recited to a few friends that signed their author's death warrant.
Obviously, I don't have the slightest intention of comparing myself
        to Mandelstam
or to any other poet writing within rifle shot of deadly auditors
nor, for that matter, to Muhammad ibn al-Dheeb al-Ajami,
recently sentenced to life in prison (subsequently reduced to a
        mere 15 years)
for reciting a poem on YouTube that displeased the Emir of Qatar.

I can't imagine any poem I might write coming with such a price.
yet I live at a time when writing and its surveillance
have become practically synonymous.
In *Discipline and Punish* (original French title, *Surveiller et Punir*)
Foucault cites Bentham's panopticon prison
where an inmate can't know whether or not he or she
is being watched by a guard at any given moment
so must assume that observation is continual.
In the present state of "carceral society" surveillance really is continual
and increasingly it is undertaken by the subjects themselves.
Fitbit, I read, is a small device to track your physical activity or sleep.
You can wear the device all day because it easily clips in your pocket,
pants, shirt, bra, or to your wrist when you are sleeping.
The data collected is automatically synched online when the device
is near the base station. After uploading, you can explore visualizations
of your physical activity and sleep quality on the web site.
You can also view your data using their new mobile web site.
You can also track what you eat, other exercises that you do,
      and your weight.

This is the world prophesied by Kenneth Goldsmith circa 1997
when he submitted himself to week-long audio surveillance
or attempted to describe his every physical action for a
      13-hour period.
It's also the world embraced by a new generation of digital literary scholars
who employ data-mining techniques pioneered by the NSA.
True, poets have been engaged in "self tracking" for a long time.
"Let no thought pass incognito and keep your notebook
as strictly as the authorities keep their register of aliens," Walter
      Benjamin advised.
They've also sometimes operated on the other side of the fence:
Wordsworth spying for England on his and Coleridge's 1798
      trip to Hamburg,

Basil Bunting working undercover for British Military Intelligence
in Teheran until he was expelled in 1952.
But more often they have been the ones spied upon,
like Hugh MacDiarmid hounded in wartime Scotland
as a Communist agitator while he looked for "a poetry of facts."
At least he had the opportunity to lash back in a letter
to one of his tormentors, a certain Captain Joke Hay:
"It is intolerable that I should be subjected to inconvenience
and misrepresentation by a fatuous blowhard like you
and I have no intention of submitting to it,
even though the seriousness of it is mitigated by the fact
you are known as a windy ass and egregious buffoon
and not taken seriously by anyone who knows you."
(Andrew McNeillie, "A Scottish Siberia," *TLS*, Sept. 13, 2013.)

In *The Prelude*, Wordsworth was baffled at "how men lived
Even next-door neighbours, as we say, yet still
Strangers, not knowing each other's name."
Now I know the names of a thousand "friends" I've never met, and
        they mine,
so what do I have to hide from any device capturing these lines
to a distant database? My mind is filled with eavesdroppers and spies.
I think a thousand times, or not a second, before I commit to a phrase
and leave trails of metadata I'm asked to believe no one will ever pursue.
Rather than wallow in outmoded subjectivities
raw and naked to those unseen allseeing eyes
maybe it's better to simply claim existing chunks of language
as MacDiarmid did in the Shetland Islands in the early 1940s
transcribing lengthy passages from the *TLS*
for his eventually abandoned megapoem
"Cornish Heroic Song for Valda Trevlyn."
In June 1940 the authorities judged him "a case for continued observation"
and in the following March put him on the "invasion list."

"It is probably unnecessary," Brooman-White wrote to Major
        Peter Perfect
(Box 5, Edinburgh) on March 16, 1941, "as no doubt the local Police
        and Military
are all standing round waiting to pounce on him,
but to make assurance doubly sure, it might be as well to have his
        name added.
I think we have plenty of evidence to justify this
but if you like I will send you up a summary of our file against the man."

The character Iris Henderson (Margaret Lockwood) in Hitchcock's
        The Lady Vanishes,
released in 1938, the year Mandelstam died,
having tea in the dining car with the charming
but penniless musicologist Gilbert Redman (Michael Redgrave)
when she glimpses the name that Miss Froy (Dame May Whitty)
had left on the window, a second before it vanishes.
She bolts from the table and desperately addresses the travelers
        around her:
"I appeal to you, all of you—stop the train. Please help me.

Please make them stop the train. Do you hear?
Why don't you do something before it's too late?"
Redgrave and duplicitous psychiatrist Dr. Harz (Paul Lukas)
attempt to restrain her but she breaks away.
Before pulling the train's emergency cord and collapsing in
        a dead faint,
she cries out: "I know! You think I'm crazy, but I'm not.
For heaven's sake, stop this train. Leave me alone. Leave me alone."
Amid the fascist shadows she is driven to hysteria
because a text has vanished before it could acquire other readers.

At the Whitney's "Rituals of Rented Island"
I walk into the Squat Theater installation, suddenly remembering
evenings of radical performance circa 1979
as a long-forgotten line from one of Kafka's parables
hisses around me in low-fi analog:
"Nobody could fight his way through here even with a message from
    a dead man."

ANGE MLINKO

ERIC ARTHUR BLAIR

George Orwell barely escaped the vortex in the Gulf
of Corryvreckan, called Charybdis Brecani by St. Adamnan.
To take the name Orwell keeps the whirlpool close.

These Lacassine cities grew out of loathing: Opelousas,
prettier than a row of crape myrtles the grazing horses.
George Orwell barely escaped the vortex. In the Gulf,

the Gator Chateau, near Evangeline, serves Hurricanes.
Calcisieu: a kid's throwing bottle caps at the fuel pumps;
the fizz of it keeps the whirlpool close.

Trucks haul carnival rides, coils of chain link fencing,
portable generators. An army convoy goes by;
who knows if they escaped the vortex in the Gulf.

A washed dollar comes up pale fuschia, like a spoonbill.
In these parts, fuschia blooms without hoopla
but its radial symmetry keeps the whirlpool close.

The cormorants shuffle feathers like a deck,
then land on the stern where coil the ropes.
George Orwell barely escaped the vortex in the Gulf.
To take the name Orwell keeps the whirlpool close.

PAULA CISEWSKI

SUPER MOON REPORT

Sun Yung Super-Moon-gazed
from Stone Arch Bridge with
a hundred other gazers. Underneath,

the swelled Mississippi continued
leaving. In a basement lounge hidden
from the sky, Paul D. cracked

open a can of PBR and made
a toast to a lost friend.
Our cities were recovering from a storm.

Laura closed her eyes and swayed
with the tide while reciting
a rock star Super Moon set.

Many of our oldest trees had fallen.
Rudy and Zaeva used the Super Moon glow
as a flashlight until electricity

was restored. Smart kids
with their orbiting toy.
If Dobby cracked it open,

I imagine he found a fortune
inside the Super Moon.
The Super Moon's in Capricorn,

said Sarah, giving me a knowing look.
A Capricorn, I was waiting to feel some effects.
The moon outshone the stars in an ink-pure heaven.

Strangers were living in shopping malls temporarily
which was hard to believe in this calm.
The Capricorn Super Moon will expose

government corruption! said Jack, who also knows
a bit about astrology. But then
it'll get charged with espionage and flee

the country! said Fred, who knows
about current events. John said nothing.
His stormless moon-glowing

was a kind of earthly home. Everyone
felt down-sized by the extra moon and the extra weather.
Those present on the illuminated sidewalk

embraced before parting ways. Then, here and there
on our hemisphere, the Super Moon
became a facebook meme.

It doesn't seem that much closer,
read a lot of status updates, and
all the attached Super Moon phone photos

resembled anemic second cousins.
All the faces down below all the satellites
lit up in the night by all the love

and all the storms
and all the screens.
And the something-like-comfort

of knowing the one who misses you most
is home tweeting about
the moon you just admired, alone.

KEN BABSTOCK

FROM *PERFECT BLUE DISTANT OBJECTS*

Standing here not in advance
of doubt, thinking a man favours sight

that he forget objects, the visible many come
before he tastes a mature will,

either his smell is moderated by
the hood or time in any

distant region, coursing through various
severed happenings, has eaten two different

things. These never before nor since,
pleasant but scarce, pleasant because scarce.

We altered much to have reason to
taste the impulse of the singular, though

repeating such certainty in servers
is decidedly a taste seen in things. Things

have a precision, a more visual memory
of once having been here only once.

In Holland they can smell
the peculiar city of Now. These odours

place ideas of I in the vivid remainder.
With interest, they repeat the forms of sensation:

A mere twenty took the isle of Jamaica.
Now perhaps the fruit of certainty

is added to periodic ideas
of visual retention, losses proven

in time's distant objective, various
delicate families during years

sensation used hands to know itself,
conveying the effects of boys trying

to call out for light. I cannot be several
left in a weak man's shade.

Better they survey what they can;
war is an actuality they refer to as proof.

JOSHUA CLOVER

VERSIONS

Three versions exist
of *Workers Leaving
The Lumière Factory.*

The one horse,
two horse, and
no horse versions.

The workers are
mostly female and
their clothes change

according to the
seasons. The film
is in the

public domain. As
are the workers
now. Work is

not itself in
the public domain
also known as

the market that
ends where the
factory gates begin.

I immediately feel
the warmth of
the workers and

proletarians again every
time I don
the ski mask

said Toni Negri.
The Return to
Work at the

Wonder Factory also
captures them outside
the building, the

workers I mean,
in the public
domain on camera.

They have voted
to go back
into that shithole

but the woman
says we're all
black from it,

the pretty boss
is in the
office, the woman

with hair like
Anna Karina says
no no no.

Some preliminary notes.
We become visible
when leaving work.

In the market
one must appear.
The black mask

resembles the factory:
it isn't public.
We wish to

end them both.
The black bloc
wants to move

toward the condition
of being numerous,
so much that

masks become unnecessary
at which time
we will see

that it comprises
neither "outside agitators"
nor some specially

privileged bunch of
white boys — per
the dovetailing stories

of right media
and left counterrevolutionaries —
but is everyone.

The faces of
women and men
and of others

the faces of
friends and of
strangers—their appearance

in open air
at the end
of public and

private, at the
far end of
market and factory,

will not be
the triumph of
visibility, of the

theology of transparency,
but its total
and crushing defeat.

THERA WEBB

ORTHICON

Admit, we darken everything we touch, and there's no power left in a moth wing caught between candle and glass, or ivory torn at the root. It's broken mirror, a dead bird crawling out of a flaming egg, a smoking scar up the side of the mountain. We're barely animal. Trapped in an airplane globed in light, the wind a dancing dog around us, we breathe in measured air, our faces flashed across a city's thousand screens. We're cattled and controlled. In the files we're blackened ink, a filament resisting light.

Unspool this tape, unedit, write me like I'm not inside this skin.

VICTORIA CHANG

THE BOSS LOOKS OVER US

The boss looks over us the boss likes us the boss
　　　　irks us hurts us the boss smiles
　　at us smirks at us the boss lies to us confirms
　　　　her offer of employment the boss

gives us provides us deploys us the boss
　　　　accommodates us no animus no
　　animal no nitpick she picked us and her and
　　　　her to knit together we tried to

knit my father back together
　　　　starting with *I am Victoria I am*
　　your daughter you have two daughters I am I can
　　　　I have to be knitted back together

I am a flaw *a burst of passion or a passing wind*
　　　　in an office a burst of passion can
　　only lead to the door out the door down
　　　　the stairs through another door into

the passionate wind where there once used to sit
　　　　a metal bull near a fountain with a gold sphere
　　and people eating lunch people eating benches people
　　　　covered with lungs and dust

THE BOSS WOULD LIKE TO SEE US

The boss would like to see us not in person
            but would like to see us do something
        better the boss would like to see us see ourselves
            differently would like to see if

we can do something one way her way that way
            I take out the sign and turn the arrow
        the other way another one comes in is hired to see
            if something can be executed to see if

others can be muted if someone can be
            refuted looted electrocuted another one
        comes in and turns around and walks out on the way
            out another one looks at us calls us

brave the group is scared the group no longer wants
            to be groped the group scores me strokes
        me scores points by being silent the boss's hair
            looks like lint it turns grey then

greyer her hair hugs me envies me for being
            brave not a slave for being free
        of the boss my eyebrows for being shaped
            like birds that think they can fly away

FENG CHEN

YOU DON'T KNOW WHAT LOVE IS

irony came to me in the cradle and left a scar on my forehead
in grandiose dilutions I am Harriet Potter in monolids
monologues do not occur to me but when I am wounded the
    wounds weep
Harriet, you are the object of infinite gazes
the scope of survival is also infinite
when the universe has morphed into a fruit fly's eye
and every little pustule of sight is an ideology shattered
maybe Pussy Riot is right
but in the cold eye of a dead lover who is the sun, the moon, the scars
when you are a woman slowly putrefying into your original state of
    monstrosity
no one controls the truth of capital or suffering
ignorance pads you in its soft institution
and will not let you die
my brother says, think of moss and ivy growing on a wall
and I think of Juliette's survey of Damnation
beauty survives life, hope, humanity itself
moss and ivy covers a slice of ruin that continues to disintegrate
    like a scene
moss and ivy a film that slowly proliferates all over white noise
all over the masterpiece of white noise and white hot
    white novelty
Wanda Coleman is dead
she grows like ivy, Romeo
I am watching chinese tv through parental satellites
but have no comment or insight on the hyperfast morphology
    that stretches

the width of chinese women's eyes, every music video strident,
     ahistorical and estranged
self yellowface speaking of China's modernity
I tell my friends that a root canal is leaking terror into my body
it has been leaking since adolescence
when I love yourselves through the devil's door I die and move as
     a brilliant corpse
until they retreat
suddenly, the false aura of auras behind every empty object
suddenly muffed
and my dead soil is revealed, the flesh ambitious with beauty, that despair
destiny out of my dead hands,
I await the gods
Harriet, we are depending on you to shoulder the burden of salvation

EILEEN G'SELL

I LIKE THAT YOU DON'T CARE ABOUT MONEY

I am someone who's good with money. I know where it is and where it's not. I know how to save it, how to spend it, how to earn it all back the day it's gone. I don't like that I am good with money because I do not like the money itself. I am good with money the same way I am good with workaholics, the way I'm good with supersad people who often want to die, the way I'm good with sore losers and good with oral surgery and good with lo-calorie kettle corn. I am not sure you are good with money. You sleep like it does not exist. It's the same as if I believed in God, believed He watched my every move, but you were one of those merry atheists who don't know anyone's watching. I'm watching you. I want to learn, to be good with someone very good. I would give you all my money if you gently asked me for it, but I'd also surely make a lot more of it once you're gone. Once one learns what is gone, being good with gone is worthless. Once you're gone is important—would surely cost a lot.

MATTHEW ZAPRUDER

HOW DO YOU LIKE THE UNDERWORLD

The completely to me magical screen
sits in the middle of this black desk,
the one I put together with such trouble,
following the instructions, muttering
its nonsensical Swedish name like a spell.
The screen is a dark window.
It can be made slowly light
by pushing a single button. It nobly rises,
a monument to a process begun
some years ago in a completely
dust free facility thousands of miles
from Oakland where the free sun
beats gently down on the heads
of my neighbors. I hear them
now for two sunlit moments pause
to converse as their dogs touch noses.
Meanwhile in the factory the workers
wear white dust proof suits.
The boss watches from a catwalk above.
To be troubled only abstractly
by the thought the thought in me
of those totally pure white clad
very real workers makes me
a kind of boss
though I wish I were not
is the ultimate white person problem.
To solve it I would like to ask
an ancient philosopher, preferably one in a cave.

But they are extinct. The humans
who are not robots at all
are right now robotically putting together
insanely precise atomic components
that make what we do go.
Thus I can watch and interact
with people I call followers or friends.
Or rather the words they have put together.
Down the screen they scroll.
It makes me so dizzy.
For a while I watched and thought,
how interesting. Then sad
thinking animals. Without a thought
to make them close
I closed my eyes and saw
a monk reading a book in the garden.
The book was about music others
left for us long ago and departed.
What can you learn
from a book about music?
Some say to settle for winter.
But they have read way too much Rilke,
he is very dead, and his problems
though cosmic did not include
the round earth becoming hotter.
I heard somewhere in Africa
they have found a glittering valley
an asteroid crashed into millions of years ago
and filled with useful silicate.
The frustules i.e. shells of single cell
diatoms make a white earth
you can pack into tiny packets
to keep things dry on their journeys
to our stores. I bought some
at Grand Lake Ace Hardware to combat

the tiny harmless ants that plagued me.
They plague me no more.
It's time for the patriots to move forward.
Let's go live now to that lake.
The smooth black totally ichthyic
divers plunge. To watch them
and wonder is like donning
the ceremonial oven mitts and trying
to grab a black coin in a darkened basement.
Beautiful pre middle aged people,
right now in the uncountable moments
interposed between us and lunch
together we sleepwalk
in the best interest of claws.
We have broken the future of thunder.
Is it interesting or sad? There is no difference.
All children's books are now about death.

ZACH SAVICH

NEIGHBORHOOD WATCH

(1)

Trail maintained by flood. Flood maintained by everything.

Asked my neighbors—they know I teach at an art school—would they mind for one week recording every time they saw me, just in the ordinary course of things, when was it, what was I doing. Gave each a notepad, pen, pulpy detective novel. We talked casually about drones, metadata, surveillance. How does it change when you are an instrument of information, when the gathering of information becomes the creation of further information (because of how information is processed/analyzed), so no one is a primary or important character ("let them read my emails!") because we have already been totalized (nullified) by indiscriminate data-izing.

Left town for a week, came to see each when I was back, some apologized for not seeing me, one said he saw me come home with beer Tuesday night, one said she'd grown worried. I apologized and said there'd been an urgent family thing. She apologized and asked if I needed more help with my school project. Her son had been in Iraq. He comes around some times with his small daughter. She likes to pile things on the sidewalk in front of the house. Shoes, plastic comb, rocks.

Turn around often on the way in so you'll know what it will look like coming back. If you don't come back at least you'll have an idea of how it might have seemed.

(2)

One neighbor always stared hard through the front window, so we put the inflatable dummy in the window and I sat at my usual place at the table—would she feel "caught" in the dummy's gaze and thus swivel from observer to observed and look away or perhaps stare harder? No observable difference, two days trial. Moved dummy to the table with me.

In the parking lot past our backyard the other night, a guy shouting. You think it's a fight then realize he's on the phone and whoever he is shouting at must love him very much to not hang up or else is shouting the same.

(3)

Month it must be getting lighter earlier—the lights along the tracks (on a sensor) have started turning off earlier than the lights outside the station café (on a timer).

Took to sitting on the bench outside the station and when the 5:36 came from Center City I'd disperse with the train crowd up the residential streets leading to Germantown Ave. Often I'd been reading on the bench, so I felt that our motion through the streets resembled what was happening to words in my brain. Selected one regular commuter (middle-aged, white, tall, balding, long overcoat on his arm) not to follow but to walk ahead of, taking a slightly different route each day (or, really, not remembering which route I had taken on any other day) and at some point turning a corner and abruptly stopping, waiting to see if he would turn the corner and we would finally meet.

Waiting for the morning train I like to stand where I can see the couple from up the street arrive with their dogs, talk for a minute, kiss goodbye, and he leaves with both the dogs and she comes over to the tracks. I don't think they are happier than we are.

CARRIE OEDING

SHH, DON'T WAKE UP THE PAINTINGS

Sometimes I want to be everything but impressive. My walk is artless. A common duck, always unfilmed. I am always waiting to be. I am always.

Impressed, I pace the artist in my neighborhood who walks with a busted can of paint. A line of paint following him, he only looks forward.

I like his emotions. There are none. Perhaps many. Nobody watches what we're doing. Like I have permission to get it wrong.

All I ever used to do was wait to be moved. And be told what to do. Now I fear this is how I'm going to impress you.

I hope the age of *Is It Art or Not?* is becoming *Want to Go For a Walk?*

I have feelings, I write them about people. Does that mean I have to live in the suburbs?
I fall in line with an artist, so maybe you think I live somewhere worth something.

I have students without teeth and safety. Our tap water is a gimmick in a postmodern plot. Our mayor promotes deer hunting from sidewalks. There's a bullet hole through the little bell on my cat's collar.

Between thinking and action there should be a bell. But we lost the little ball that makes that bell jangle.

I already broke into sincerity and no one seemed to care. I was free to touch the art and swim in the pool unattended.

JOE HALL

FROM *DOMESTIC SURVEILLANCE*

Subject: Cheryl Quimba
Date: 8/14/12
Time: 11:07 am

Her mini-laptop on a bamboo table mat. The note Jeanie wrote on the back of a business card:

Bureau Veritas
bureauveritas.com
-career
-customer support
-inspections

xxxxxxx.xxxx@gmail.com

I put the card beside the mat. The card was the bookmark she was using when reading in the guest bed. She told me to put the card on the kitchen table.

The table: two mugs. One mug with red-orange letters:

I BET
I
CAN

3/8ths full of filtered water. A few clouds of lime pulp floating in this water. More pulp on the mug's bottom. The smudge of a drip dried over the letter E. The ridges and grooves of her fingers worked in oil, print overlapping print, around the mug which is between two clay tea cups— the handles of both cups face toward the center of the table, away from the wall which the table is against. Also beside the wall, in line with the 2 mugs, her small black notebook, a yellow square of adhesive note paper on the notebook, a pen nested along the notebook's pages. Her orchid.

Five pairs of shoes on or pushed under a rack. Two pairs of sandals, two of tennis shoes, one of flats. On one pair of tennis shoes the laces are tied at the 3rd of 5 eyes in a knot I don't understand—the shoelace itself is full of smaller knots mending where the shoelace was broken.

The curtains she closed.

The foyer blackboard:

$2 shared money to C
turmeric root
almond milk

The bathroom. On my side of the sink everything but toothpaste. The end of the toothpaste on her side, this end falling across the center of the sink, cap on my side. 3 hair pins on the top of the sliding mirror, the bend of each pin toward the ledge. The worn-down bristles of a toothbrush. The crescents of black hairs crisscrossing the tiles beneath the sink on one wall and the toilet on the other. A shaving from a pencil. The dust of her skin.

The bedroom door ajar. A black plastic hanger on the outer knob. A chair my grandfather made in the corner, by the air conditioner and radiator. A silk scarf with paisley flowers over the chair back. An olive, hooded sweatshirt over its arm, the hood in the lap of the chair, the flowered seat cushion—the flowers somewhere between unpeeling irises and loose petunias. The head of a skin brush on the cushion. The detached handle deeper in the seat of the chair. In the chair, all the way back, a poem she wrote and framed with cardboard wrapped in fabric. The string that hung the poem on doors in Indiana and Baltimore is missing.

Comforter pulled up near the pillows. Folds and runs in the comforter, small hill over the pillow under it, near the center of the bed.

Man's boxer shorts and tan shirt she sleeps in.

Nightstand: *Autobiography of Alice B Toklas*, the little booklet Aimee assembled from the paper she made over a small sheaf of poems, a tin box that reads "Mrs. McGregor's Family Nail Box. Manufactured by American Steel & Wire Co., Chicago: New York: Cleveland: Pittsburgh: Denver." Two quarter-sized clumps of silicon. Binder clip. Nightstand's lower shelf: a box of checks, *Siddhartha*.

Beside the nightstand, behind the gauzy curtains, a photograph of her and her sister, who is missing. The subject sits in a swing with her hands folded over the wooden lap bar, not smiling. Her sister stands up, the seat of the swing at her waist, her hands on this seat, not smiling but with a playful expression. Behind her is a wall made of cinderblock, sun bleached dirt and weeds.

A flower Aimee folded from paper and sewed into a rectangle of blue. Along the flower's stem cursive words: *Once I learned the word Utopia / I never had to look it up.*

Basket of laundry by desk lamp on the floor.

MICHAEL EARL CRAIG

THE COUPLE

She threw her Thomas Bernhard books at him,
it took eight or nine minutes.
Then she left, running over him with her Yukon.
The cigarette she'd thrown down
smoked itself without fanfare
in the crushed gravel of the footpath.

My binoculars make a small gap in the living room curtains.

He rolls over in the drive, onto his back,
and tries to wiggle his toes, but cannot.
Oh the day does darkle, he thinks…
right away wondering about his use of darkle.
But the day *is* darkling.
Oh yes indeed, indubitably it darkles.

ANTHONY MCCANN

PRODIGALS

Do the spent later return
because they'd forgotten something? Food?
Beneath the barrel of leaves
they thought the god would drool

or something, to see them
torn from this book.
But must we go on with these Swarms of the Judge
Horsebacked, Bewhipped, Pommelhand-Drawn

and the way they fix me
in gaze with the ranch?
Perhaps I would never—
and the barrel, the fence.

Like when riding in the hills
one tosses back one's head...
But now, the night, and jasmine unfold
and the land gets promised

to someone at the end.
Meantimes, I, the poet, have returned from nearby
to be far away from you
with you and all my words.

But now you have the words—
with the little pictures they arrive,
to be near you, inside you
just when they disappeared. You'll see here a small deer

in the arms of the erased. Here is the river
where the capture of the deer, and the
forest and the war and the vast
gray poisoned lake. Meanwhile the light is changing,

rolling down the sky
to a lot, behind a fence, with the weeds
and now the stumps. Feathered, pre-historic,
we are drying in their throats

and are echoed, and brought further,
over distance, by the doves.
But will you buy what I have bought,
will you hold it to your zone

and smell it with your lips
while I squeak on you like doves—
"I, in this symphony of god
am your head, I am drowning your head"

that's what their song said.
But here our bodies turned away, each burrowed toward its core,
and the image that was there and flickered
and went on. Riding back

in the truck, white leaves poured overhead
like song words in light rain
till the strategy devolved
and at dawn we were possessed,

like in the frieze or photograph,
on the patio   and damned
with ornamental froth.
So the god turned us into furniture

in its songs about the past.
You've been squirming for three minutes now
with its words under your flesh,
stuck into your skin, by this radiant quack.

And the cheese on the counter grows wet and more sick,
and the news day is slick
with more thoughtless heat.
But then the birds began in unison:

"why lock up your throats"
one can start again, there are gestures between thoughts,
a slipping out of pants, and into different dress:
a mustache and a wing—and every Tuesday add a tusk,

or painted goiter on the hip
out by the foam-injected stones.
But then life caught up with us again
and then two years and then the war

beneath the surface of our jobs,
as the light will rise and fall
on the patch of dirt we made,
to which we'd sworn to turn away,

and grow tubers and a school
of congealed light and noise.
Staggering now, with nothing like a will,
we round the corner of that house

and burst onwards towards home.
Then Day, so friendly sometimes, so sometimes
far away, on the hillside with the forehead rocks
and the tiny golden birds, appeared

on all the roadways, on the grass patches
with the shrubs, in the trees
that money placed, next to the on-ramp
in the swamp. I remember once under those trees,

while inside our bones grew dark,
cars whooshed and rubber flaked
along the edges, with the light.
It was of the edges the light spoke

and of the shapes preceding names
that flew in patterns through our lungs:
a wren, I thought, *a face.* "Birdbath,"
you said, and straight out of that bush

a hummingbird rose at a speed beyond breath.
Another one born, shrinking, lifted up.
It's all, as the song goes,
too beautiful for votes.

The light gestures again at the longing for delay
as well as the devotion to arrival and change.
But this curtain of forms, California,
is a fetish for all kinds of enforcers

who wield the pulsing blob of lines
by which we are each removed from the earth.
Are persons like ours really needed
to carry these bodies and eyes?

And so back again to the city
and the red flow, from vents,
of the names. Buried under the house
with our umbilical cords and our names

we're alone again in their dream.
This was the meaning of catch and release.
But the very next day charm returned,
as the true source of life as we knew it: charm of the lips,

our charming limbs, a movement of voice
and the lids. So in our caskets
we left rods and sticks
and hid out again in the trees.

It's this need for adventure in everyday life,
to take the wrong turn in the park
and discover the forest they left there
where men suck each other and fuck. That lake

is covered in soundproofing and the hawks here
are smaller and fleet. They jet between pines,
then squawk, and soar out over the ridge and the cars.
I think they have multiple souls; or

I think we have multiple souls.
I see us down there in the gulch
with the streaming light and the mud
when we stared at the birch long enough

to begin to sprout leaves in your blood.
But nighttime's home improvement
draws us out again from the trees
over the lawns, helplessly houseward,

and the neighbors rush inside.
So we vote for more darkness,
tall grass, and more wind: moon-rise over the damned.
Let this moment stand for me, myself,

addressed to you, paused in the doorway
at the trauma near the end. The shadow
of my hat falls flat across my face, obscuring
all the features there. And you, in the ski-mask

smirking in the hall—what will happen next?
So taking care to wipe the knobs
we padded backwards down the stairs;
the neighborhood had vanished

in the mirrors and the screens. Night beat against our hips
like bodies in a gym. It was as if we could proceed
unarmed into the woods and there
find a bed of furs and feathers in the dirt

and resting there and dreaming
regain our bodies and their limbs
and then emerge along the wires that led back into the mall.
And so we'd see you there, on the corner

at the light, face shadowed by your hoodie,
leaning on the oak, when we passed
in borrowed cars on our way to get more drugs.
Rewind the film, repeat, watch the bellies of the leaves

in slow motion lifted up by speed and then the wind.
First the wind, then the grass, then the words began to tick
and the next thing that I touched was your body on the screen.
But soon a less personal question arose—

that of loneness...touching the food...
How to explain it to others
in your bathrobe driving west to a sound
or dazed by a jade plant at noon?

The colors are perfect but the lines are unreal
for the dreamless afflicted by roadsigns and blur.
Still, if over each object at once each of our bodies inclines,
and if the words of description each utters

shake through the bodies and air,
can't we say that the object is singing, that its absence,
like presence, is there? It's like it was in the beginning
in the world back on the farm.

The hungry shapes were willing—the barrels and the boats.
Love in the foreground would trace a twisted bough,
and in the glitter on the ice, that vanishment was yours.
The others gathered there in families

at the edges, at the shore. Is there any hope for us at all, they said.
Not for us, they said.
So coming back now from the North,
Life foretold itself again, bloviated, blank,

on top of all this. Take it with you, please,
like a photo of these chairs
impersoned on the dock
and left there with the years.

DAN CHELOTTI

ANGELS

       show up at the moment
of the fuck up to watch. Angels also
show up at the death of everyone.
I learned this from the movies.
Busy, the watchers.
Ever since I flushed my friend's frog,
I tried throughout childhood
to switch off the camera that had
been following me around.
I failed so I forgot it. Now, I don't
sense its presence during bootleg
kisses or while I stand hunched
over a calculator. Only when I come
here to this candle lit room
with the record player under
the snowy window in the house
by the lake does the eye in the wall
open. What have you been doing,
it asks. I walk outside to watch
the beautiful view hum that song
I used to hum and turn my hat
against the wind. The moon is
beautiful. The lake. I crush my
Cigarette and turn toward the sliding
door. Haven't done much, I say.
Sure you have, it says.

LENSES

It's been years since I watched
The Conversation,
a movie about watching others
through a lens. The technology
in that film is outdated,
but outside of art, what isn't?
Humans haven't been able
to look at each other without
lenses for a while now,
but as each of us walks away
from a really good date
intentionally breathing
in the night that is filled
with the breath of others,
we for a moment lower
our lenses and drink the primordial air.
Friends, let's hook arms and sing,
The world, older than any of us,
is still young.

✖✖✖✖✖✖✖✖✖✖✖✖✖✖✖✖\ INDEX /✖✖✖✖✖✖✖✖✖✖✖✖✖✖✖✖

⟩⟨⟩⟨⟩⟨⟩⟨ ACKNOWLEDGMENTS ⟨⟩⟨⟩⟨⟩⟨⟩

The poets, for their brave and wonderful contributions. Deb Chasman, Daniel Pritchard, Timothy Donnelly, and Simon Waxman at *Boston Review* for their ideas and guidance. Janaka Stucky for his support. The websites, periodicals, projects, and presses that first published some of these poems, particularly *The Awl*, *Berfrois*, Bon Aire Projects, *Boston Review*, *Gulf Coast*, *London Review of Books*, McSweeney's Poetry Series, PEN Poetry Series, *Sou'wester*, *Virginia Quarterly Review*, *The Walrus*, and Wave Books. Mary Burchenal, Karen Harris, and my parents for the joy of reading poetry.